Mark G. Worster

JONES MEDIA
PUBLISHING

Jones Media Publishing
10645 N. Tatum Blvd. Ste. 200-166
Phoenix, AZ 85028
www.JonesMediaPublishing.com

Disclaimer:

The author strives to be as accurate and complete as possible in the creation of this book, notwithstanding the fact that the author does not warrant or represent at any time that the contents within are accurate due to the rapidly changing nature of the Internet.

While all attempts have been made to verify information provided in this publication, the Author and the Publisher assume no responsibility and are not liable for errors, omissions, or contrary interpretation of the subject matter herein. The Author and Publisher hereby disclaim any liability, loss or damage incurred as a result of the application and utilization, whether directly or indirectly, of any information, suggestion, advice, or procedure in this book. Any perceived slights of specific persons, peoples, or organizations are unintentional.

In practical advice books, like anything else in life, there are no guarantees of income made. Readers are cautioned to rely on their own judgment about their individual circumstances to act accordingly. Readers are responsible for their own actions, choices, and results. This book is not intended for use as a source of legal, business, accounting or financial advice. All readers are advised to seek the services of competent professionals in legal, business, accounting, and finance field.

Printed in the United States of America

ISBN: 978-1-945849-96-1 paperback
JMP2020.3

DEDICATION

For my mother Evelyn Call Worster,
who shared so many lessons in her time,
the greatest of which was to love everyone,
regardless of circumstance and social standing.
For you, Mom.

CONTENTS

AUTHOR'S PREFACE

I began writing this book in January 2019 after selling all my possessions the year prior and moving to Brooklyn, New York, to begin a new chapter in my life with an amazing woman. Fortunately, life for me is composed of unexpected twists and turns. What seems like heartbreak sometimes proves to be the catalyst for amazing transformation. I found myself in that place of intense introspection and transformation. This book is the outcome of that cathartic introspection, and it is the first of many on the subject of being alive—I mean really being alive.

Through this process of deep introspection, I was able to bring together forty years of self-help programs, therapy, and meditative experience to answer the question, Why do we do the things we do?

The writing was agonizingly slow until November 2019. In November I attended a seminar called "Being a Master of Life: What It Takes" in London offered by the personal development company Landmark Worldwide. The seminar was presented by Dr. Joseph DiMaggio, senior executive overseeing the research, development, and design team for Landmark; and Werner Erhard, founder of EST (Erhard Seminars Training), the precursor to Landmark Worldwide. For one powerful weekend, five hundred diverse individuals from around the world inquired about the nature of what it truly means to be a human being. That weekend proved to be the catalyst to completing this work.

I'm grateful to Jeremy Jones from Jones Media Publishing for his patience and sage advice, and I'm extremely grateful to Chris and Trisha Merrill for the use of their home over a cold week in Newport, Rhode Island, as I completed the writing of this book at the end of December 2019.

I'm thankful I wasn't motivated to write until after the seminar; this would have been a different book had I pushed through earlier in the year. Sometimes learning to patiently wait for the moment to arrive is the best thing to do.

Acknowledgments

I'd like to acknowledge each and every person who played an active role in supporting my efforts to finish this book. You know who you are. I'm eternally grateful for you being an integral part of the tapestry of my life!

Introduction

Have you ever asked yourself why things never seem to change no matter how much you want them to?

Ever find yourself asking why all your relationships seem to end in failure?

Almost ten years ago, I came seconds away from ending my life after falling into despair. At that exact moment, I felt as if there was nothing left for me to live for.

Fast forward to today—I live the most extraordinary life. I love it! I've been accused of being the happiest guy alive, and I am. I'm surrounded by people, near and far, who truly love me for who I am; I have everything I've ever wanted.

The challenge is this—how do you fundamentally change the way you think? How do you go from "life sucks" to "life happens, good and bad, and I love it!"?

I've spent the last few (forty) years discovering the secrets to creating a life that I love and that satisfies me completely. I'll share how to enter this new reality, so that you can get started living your new life right now.

In this book you will discover and understand the following:

- How we're wired to interact with the world
- How events at an early age determine how we react to situations in life
- How to become aware of your thoughts and how to use that awareness to choose differently
- How the food we eat affects everything we do
- The power of movement in maintaining joy and happiness
- Specific daily habits to create the life you love

For me it was literally life or death; I had to change how I related to world. The result of that effort uncovered an amazing, new world available to anyone committed to living a life of joy and happiness. By the end of this book, you will understand how to create a life you've only dreamed of.

1

SETTING THE STAGE

Sometimes I wonder if suicides aren't in fact sad
guardians of the meaning of life.

Václav Havel

It was May 12, 2011, a beautiful Boston spring evening. Up until that point, I'd led a pretty damn successful life. I was running the same tech consulting company I had started in 1987; we'd had great success, having made the "Inc. 500," a list of the fastest-growing privately held companies, twice in a row at one point. I had two daughters successfully off into the world at college, and I had a son I joyfully spent all my spare time with. I was, for all intents and purposes, a happy, successful guy. I arrived home from dinner and drinks with friends, went into my bedroom, sat back on my bed, thought about my life for a minute, got up reached into my dresser drawer, slowly pulled out my shiny 9mm Smith & Wesson and put it to my head.

How did a seemingly successful, happy person get to the point where they would take their life?

At that point, I had every reason to call it quits. My ex-wife had moved my son nine hundred miles away and I never saw him, my fiancée of three years had just broken up with me and told me she found someone else, my business of twenty-five years was running in the red, and to top it all off, the biggie of big ones—my beloved seventeen-year-old nephew, who was my son's best friend, had just killed his mother, my beautiful sister-in-law, and buried her in the backyard of my brother's home, which had been our grandparents home and a place of great importance in our family. Add in a lifelong history of depression, mood swings, and alcohol abuse, the result could have been catastrophic.

And then I thought about how my children would find me: half of my head missing and parts of my brain scattered about the room. I just couldn't let that happen, so I checked myself in for a weekend stay at the local hospital lockdown unit. Thus began a journey into understanding how our stories build our reality, how our perspective on life affects what we do on a moment by moment basis.

I immediately began to practice what I had learned over forty years of self-development but had not actually put fully into action. I'm like anyone else: wired for habitual actions. I attended a seminar on habit change, where the presenter, the then head of the Neuroscience Department at Dartmouth College, said, "The good news is you can change your habits, the bad news is it's extremely difficult."

We are what we think. Our genetic nature coupled with our personal experiences dictates how we approach the world. We create stories based on experiences, and those stories operate in the background, mostly without our awareness of it. We gather evidence to support the stories and that solidifies their hold on our lives.

In his book *Escaping the Labyrinth: Body Memory—The Secret Code That Creates, Sustains, and Can Unlock Our Chains*, author David William Sohn describes how we, as humans, by the time we are five years old have already decided three things: who I am, who you are, and how the world is. These decisions become an automated script as we encounter the world. The problem is twofold: (1) we live with the decisions a five-year-old made and (2) we have no idea the script is even running in our subconscious and stored in our very cells. I don't know about you, but I love five-year-olds. We are blissfully unaware. But I certainly would not want decisions made by a five-year-old to run my life. My baseline story use to be that "I'm unlovable, you can't be trusted, and the world is judgmental." Imagine how my interaction with others was with this script running silently in the background!

Let me reiterate—we are what we think. Everything starts with what we think. What we think determines our actions.

People spend millions of dollars on self-help books and seminars (me included). I've been working on me for a long, long time. Until a few months ago, I still had my original Tony Robbins cassette tapes from his initial launch as a life coach. You name it: I've read it, listened to it, experienced it, tried to implement it in my life. All of it had a positive effect on me, without a doubt. But it was like putting lipstick on a pig. Until I was able to go back and clear up the past, since the past was consistently dragged into my future, it was all an exercise in futility. Until I uncovered the foundational stories that ran my life, the endless loop of searching for the next "right thing" to fix me would continue.

Let's start by exploring the nature of a human being. How is it that we interact with the world around us and make sense of it all?

For neuroscientists, the brain is the cause of consciousness. In their world, reality is about neurons, synapses, and neurotransmitters. In their world, we're simply a biochemical machine that responds to stimuli and releases chemicals in response. There is nothing more than that. No soul. No nonphysical entity. Simply an amazing biochemical machine. Using all our senses, we gather data and create an experience of the outside world.

What we see is real right? Not really. Seeing is believing isn't exactly accurate. Neuroscientist Beau Lotto, in his book *Deviate*, describes how, in actuality, we only see about 10 percent of what's out there in front of us. The brain makes up the other 90 percent; it fills in the missing data so to speak. Yep, seriously, we only truly see 10 percent of what we're looking at. It explains why when you first meet someone and fall in love, they're the most beautiful person you've ever seen. Six months later, they've aged terribly and don't look anything like they did. Your brain did this!

Consider that all our senses are rudimentary at best: we "hear" things as a result of the movement of molecules caused by vibrations. The sound funnels down our ear canal and causes the eardrum to move. The eardrum vibrates with sound and these vibrations travel through the ossicles to the cochlea. Fluid in the cochlea moves and causes the hair cells to bend, which in turn creates neural signals that are picked up by the auditory nerve. The auditory nerve sends these signals to the brain to be interpreted as sounds. Pretty cool, huh? Lots of room for things to be misinterpreted though.

The senses are not finite and refined. We operate as if what we hear and see is as real as real can get. The truth is that it's all a rough interpretation of what's outside of us.

If our experience of what's outside us isn't exactly real, how do we reconcile our interpretation of events? Is what we think real or fantasy?

We're all cells and chemicals creating thought, creating reality. How much can you control your thoughts or change what you think? Let's consider that you have almost no control over what you think: thoughts arise on their own, without any input from you.

I know that sounds crazy in our current world view of free will, but we're not as self-determining as you'd like to think (or as your thoughts like to think).

Take voluntary movement as an example. I decide to move my fingers to type these words. Inside my brain, in the supplementary motor cortex area, *readiness potential* builds up in *anticipation* of the movement. This occurs prior to any conscious thought of movement; that is, your brain knows—before you are consciously aware—that you want to initiate a movement and prepares for the movement in advance.

Who's controlling who here? Interesting, no?

In essence, we can make the case that we're really an amazing biochemical computer that runs programs in the background without any deliberate thought or action.

If our thoughts are not our own, then why have philosophers and thought leaders alike suggested we can control our thoughts?

That's what we'll delve into in subsequent chapters. But, here is a little preview, a little something to entice you to keep reading . . . it's not about thought control at all! You have no ability to control thoughts—but you do have the ability of being aware of your thoughts, and awareness allows you to change your focus. My friend Dandapani, a Hindu priest, says, "Where awareness goes, energy flows." That is where true power resides.

2

OM YEAH!

I have lived with several Zen masters—all of them cats.

Eckhart Tolle

Each and every morning I begin my day with meditation. I naturally come to a comfortable seated position. My body feels loose and open. There are no aches and pains; I feel no tightness anywhere. As I sit, my mind naturally calms down and my thoughts cease. I sit in an amazing state of bliss and harmony as the flow of love and light enters my body . . . yeah right! Not even close!

I mean, I'm sure there are people who have had that experience, and certainly I have had moments like this. But for me, and most people, it's not like that at all. Muscles are tight, thoughts are racing, nothing seems blissful at the moment. And that's the beauty of meditation— every experience, as in life, is a new adventure just waiting to be experienced.

Jon Kabat-Zinn, founder of the Mindfulness-Based Stress Reduction program, defines mindfulness as "paying attention in a particular way, on purpose, in the present moment, and non-judgmentally."

While running my last company, I decided, after attending the Landmark Advanced Forum Seminar, to enroll in nursing school and to dive into the world of healthcare. I've always wished to impact the world in a more direct way. I graduated in 2014 with an associate of science in nursing and completed my bachelor's degree in nursing in 2018. During that time I attended a weeklong, intensive program called "Yoga and Meditation for Healthcare Providers," where we studied all the solid scientific research that supports the benefits of yoga and meditation. In addition, I attended a wonderful yoga certification course for nurses offered by Annette Tersigni at Yoganurse.com.

Bhavani Lorraine Nelson, an instructor at the Kripalu Center for Yoga & Health, asked in a class offered during the weeklong, intensive program for healthcare providers, "What's the best meditation you can do?" Several of the participants offered up various meditative practices and she nodded and agreed, and then she simply said, "It's the one you can do consistently." That has stuck with me ever since, and I use that today. It's not about the methodology as much as the consistency. Whether it's meditation or diet or exercise, what matters most is consistency.

So, why is meditation so powerful? What about meditation is good for us human beings? Personally, mindfulness has literally saved my life. As I mentioned, I've suffered with medication-resistant depression my whole life: my symptoms aren't relieved by medication. Not that I haven't tried, mind you. I spent most of my adolescent years self-medicating, as a large number of adolescents do. It wasn't until I was in my mid to late twenties that I was formally diagnosed with depression (but that's another story). Suffice it to say that mental health treatment is a crap shoot at best.

I've quite literally tried almost every medication in an effort to "feel right," to have some relief from the roller coaster of mood swings that characterizes my particular genetic predisposition. Every single medication was either ineffective or came with side effects that I was unwilling to live with.

I first learned of mindfulness and meditation in 1998 while attending a yoga/meditation retreat at Kripalu. I was the last person you'd think would be at a yoga center, especially at that time in my life.

I had entered the Marine Corps at the age of seventeen, and during my preteen and teen years, I was very much an outdoorsman—think Jeremiah Johnson, a frontiersman movie character played by Robert Redford in *Jeremiah Johnson*. I was the epitome of a man's man.

My business at that time, a consulting company specializing in small to medium business computer and telephone technology, appeared to be extremely successful, having twice made *Inc.* magazine's list of the five hundred fastest growing private companies in the United States. But there was a problem: the bank had suddenly come in and demanded we repay a $300K line of credit in short order. I had no idea how I was going to come up with the money. Needless to say, my stress level was above a ten!

My therapist, a genius of a man named Timothy Goguen, suggested I go to Kripalu for a week of yoga and meditation training. I am forever grateful to Tim for that sage advice. That single week changed the course of my life. I returned to work focused and less reactive, and I was able to meet the demands of the bank and to continue to thrive. I'm happy to say that that company is now in its thirty-third year of operation.

I've spent the last twenty years learning about meditation, studying the various techniques, and seeking out experiences. I drank the Kool-Aid, so to speak. I believed. It wasn't until the advent of functional magnetic resonance imaging (fMRI) that the positive physical changes produced by meditation were conclusively proven.

Using fMRI, researchers can monitor blood flow and oxygenation in the brain. The theory is that when you utilize parts of your brain, the blood flow and oxygen levels increase. With that knowledge and tool, scientists in the field of brain research are now able to see and to understand the activity in the brain during various activities.

In the documentary *Free Solo*, which follows Alex Honnold's preparation and completion of rock climbing El Capitan in Yosemite National Park, Alex goes through fMRI testing. I had the pleasure of meeting Alex at a climbing event, and we chatted about his experience. In the film they describe how researchers used fMRI to try to determine why Alex is able to scale these peaks without the normal fear response expected from someone rock climbing without a rope and harness. It turns out that through the use of fMRI, they were able to see that Alex's amygdala response threshold (the amygdala is the part of the brain responsible for the fight-or-flight response to danger) was much higher than most other people. In other words, they were able to see that Alex doesn't experience fear as quickly as others. He can, and has time and time again, put himself in a position that would cause other people to panic, yet he stays as cool as a cucumber.

OK, that had nothing to do with meditation, or did it? Using fMRI, researchers have been able to see changes in the brain due to regular meditative practice. The size of the amygdala is decreased by meditation over time, which corresponds to a decrease in the automatic fight-or-flight response (Gotink et al. 2008) ¬—that is, you're able to calmly deal with issues that may have triggered a much different response in the past.

In addition, researchers are able to see changes in cortical thickness. Through mindfulness and meditation, the size of your brain actually increases.

To understand what is meant when it's said that brain size increases, let's talk about gray and white matter. *Gray matter* is neural tissue especially of the brain and spinal cord that contains nerve-cell bodies as well as nerve fibers and has a brownish-gray color. When we say the brain increases in size, we are referring to gray matter increasing in specific areas of the brain.

As we age, we begin to lose brain tissue. Our brains shrink most noticeably in the prefrontal cortex where working memory and executive decision-making occur. This is why as you age it becomes more difficult to remember things or to make complex decisions.

For the more experienced (older) readers—my age group, my people—pay attention to what I'm going to say next: In a study mentioned in an article in *The Washington Post*, researchers scanned, via fMRI, a group of meditators and nonmeditators; the results of the study clearly displayed a decrease in gray matter in the nonmeditator group, but in the group of meditators, the subjects over fifty had the *same* or *more* gray matter as a twenty-five-year-old (Schulte 2015).

Do I really need to spell it out for you? OK, maybe I do. If you don't meditate, start meditating now! (You'll find resources to get you started meditating in the chapter "Bringing It All Together" and in the appendix.)

So, beyond the physical benefits, why is meditation important? It goes back to what it means to be human. Consider this for a moment: you have no ability to control your thoughts or emotions. They occur and then you deal with them. See, you just had another thought. Did you generate that thought or did it just occur?

Here's my point—you and I are a conglomeration of cells and biological processes.

When we talk about thought and meditation, we're talking about awareness. It's all an illusion anyway. Your brain is simply neurons, synapses, and glial cells in a soup of neurotransmitters; it's all very mechanical and automated. If someone cuts open your head, there's no you. There's just all of these cells and chemicals.

Thoughts simply occur as a natural outcome of the communication process between the cells and neurotransmitters. And so, over the course of time, throughout your life, over all of the input that you get from your senses, your brain has been programmed. You may think that you control your thoughts, but it's bullshit: it's the grand illusion. You don't. Period. End of story.

That's why meditation is so important: you have no control over your own thoughts and emotions. But what you can create is an awareness of them. Do you see what I mean? You can become aware of your thoughts and the emotions that are tied to them. And at that moment of awareness, you have choice. With that choice you can direct the focus of your thoughts.

I journal every day, and it's positive journaling. As part of this daily meditation, I'll write about things that I'm grateful for. I'll write about the unlimited abundance in my life. Why do I do this? Repetition over and over again of positive input will change the physical wiring of my brain. I input positive data on a regular basis, so that I literally change the synapses and neural connections in the area of my brain responsible for mood and happiness. Meditation creates an awareness of what is really going on inside of me, and that awareness is the only thing that I'll ever be able to control.

Again, think about it. You just had a thought, right? Did you make that happen or did the thought just pop up out of nowhere? The you that you think you are isn't thinking thoughts, they are simply occurring.

Let's revisit an example from the first chapter. You "decide" to pick up your glass of water and have a sip. An area within your brain in the supplemental motor cortex creates a *readiness potential*, which is a measure of brain activity prior to voluntary muscle movement. The readiness potential manifests up to .35 seconds before you have the conscious awareness that you are going to reach for the glass (Libet et. al 1983).

I know what you're thinking: that's crazy! Right? What I'm telling you is that your brain knows that you're going to pick that glass up before you form the conscious thought. You truly have no capacity to control your thoughts.

Boom!

How's that for a dose of reality? We're all just automated machinery, biochemical machines. It's how we're built: emotions and thoughts are all part of an amazing biochemical reaction.

There is true freedom in accepting our nature. Understanding that we're all functioning with the same processes in place makes it far easier to forgive other folks' transgressions. Once you realize that they have the same total lack of control over their thoughts and emotions, it's easy to imagine that we're not so separated.

This is why meditation is so important—meditation gives you awareness, and your moments of awareness give you control over your life and who you are. You may not control your thoughts, but you can certainly choose how you interact with those thoughts and emotions. That's the magic. That's the key!

3

WHO'S IN CHARGE
HERE ANYWAY?

If a man should conquer in battle a thousand and a
thousand more, and another should conquer himself,
his would be the greater victory, because the greatest of
victories is the victory over oneself.

Buddha

From the age of twelve to the age of twenty-eight, I smoked
cigarettes. To tell the truth, I never much liked smoking. I hated every
aspect it, from the taste in my mouth to the smell on my clothes. Why
did I do it then? In the beginning, it was purely to be cool, to fit in with
my peers. Shortly after starting, though, it was all about the habit of
smoking and, of course, the highly addictive nature of nicotine. I must
have tried to quit over a hundred times before succeeding.

We humans love to live in the illusion that our almighty prefrontal
cortex is the part of the brain that influences our behavior most. The
truth is, we're ruled more by our larger, primitive brains than we are
aware. These lower regions control all our basic functions. Everything

from our autonomic processes (breathing, heartbeat, etc.) to who we choose as mates.

When's the last time you thought, "Hey, my blood pH is a little wonky, I better adjust that by releasing more calcium into my bloodstream from my bones"? Yeah, no one has thought that, but involuntary processes happen on a regular basis. There are millions of processes that go on without our even knowing it.

What's my point? Habits are lumped into that lower brain region as well. Our magnificent minds continually program habits into the system, and we move through life without ever even knowing they are in play.

Here's an example: the last time you lost power for a few hours, did you find yourself walking into a dark room and reflexively flipping the light switch? "Oh, duh." Your almighty prefrontal cortex knew the power was out, but the good old habitualizer said, "Hey, it's dark, turn the freaking lights on." It's how we're wired; it's how we survived all these years.

Or how about this example: remember when you first started driving a car? I clearly remember my first experience on the road. I was certain there was NO WAY two cars could fit by each other. I paid attention to every move I made, every possible thing that was coming at me. Fast forward a few months: the radio is blaring and I'm chatting with friends while operating this huge vehicle at breakneck speeds without a thought about driving. Seriously, what happened? My habitualizer had seen me drive enough that it registered all the things it needed to master the task. I didn't really need to think about it anymore.

How many times have you driven somewhere only to arrive and to think, "How the hell did I just get here?" Even better, ever drive past your exit on the freeway? Oh yes, you did; blew right past it because you were deep in thought. Who was driving the car? It wasn't the conscious you, it was the driver you!

Do you still want to cling to the idea that you control your thoughts? Hm OK, keep reading . . .

Our brains program us to continue doing today what we did yesterday because it worked yesterday and it will likely keep us alive today. In the distant past that meant staying out of the way of predators that would eat you for breakfast. Here's the rub though: there's no judgement with the habit-making part of your brain. It doesn't care that yesterday you spent the day sitting on the couch eating Ho Hos and watching *Lifetime*. Doesn't care at all. If the brain sees you do something consistently, it becomes an automatic habit.

Although with smoking you have that awful drug called nicotine to help things along, it's the ritual of smoking that people struggle with when trying to quit. Out of all the habits and vices I've dealt with, smoking was by far the hardest to quit.

That brings up a good point. We know some of the things we do are not good for our health, yet we continue to do them. It's often the case that bad habits are aided by the underlying drug within the product: nicotine, caffeine, and alcohol all have addictive qualities that, in addition to the underlying habits of use being formed, also trigger an addictive response, a dopamine rush so to speak.

Dopamine is the neurotransmitter responsible for a wide variety of feelings within a human being. It also plays a part in regulating our movement; for example, folks who have Parkinson's disease exhibit how dopamine, or the lack thereof, causes issues with movement; Parkinson's is related to the death of cells in the brain responsible for producing dopamine. Dopamine also urges us to seek things that reward us with pleasure, such as drugs, eating, and sex. Whatever pleasurable thing we do is reinforced in our brain by dopamine. It's why addiction is so difficult to treat. That consistent activation of the reward system is hard to turn off.

Why do I bring all this up? If we're not in control of our thoughts, if we are creatures of habit and we're wired for stimulation and reward, how in the hell do we deal with this reality? How do we get beyond the physiology of being human to create a life we love?

It comes back to awareness again, folks! Awareness and acceptance that we humans are a biochemical machine. Once we're aware of our nature, it's much easier to get to a point of acceptance. Once we accept that we have little control over our behavior, it's also easier to understand why others act the way they do. Our awareness opens up a world of understanding, a world of acceptance, a world of forgiveness.

Once I fell madly, hopelessly, and completely in love with the most amazing woman I had ever met. It was a fall-head-over-heels-and-drop-everything kind of love. We immediately moved in together and started making plans for our future. We also started to work together in her business. There was no question in my mind that I had finally found the one. Talk about a dopamine and serotonin flood. Wowza!

The sex? Omg! It was the best, most passionate ever! It was as if we were soul mates, connected as closely as two people could ever be. It seemed as if my dreams had come true. My search was over. This was it.

Of course, I immediately moved to the next stage—put a ring on it. It makes perfect sense. Why wait when you know this is it? (You may have a sense now that I typically go all-in when I find something I love.)

Alas, what started in January was over by the end of September. What the hell happened between January and September? What was it that caused the whole thing to blow up?

It is very simple: I had no idea that I was operating with a whole set of preconceived stories about what it means to be in a relationship, about what it means to be human. I had no idea that we are hardwired to have thoughts and emotions in a very predetermined fashion.

I thought that if I sacrificed everything in my life and became what she wanted in a man, she'd naturally reciprocate with exactly what I expected from my partner. I assumed that she would innately know what I wanted when I wanted it. How's that for expectations. How's that for setting the whole thing up for failure!

This wasn't the first time this had happened. As I dove deeply into why the relationship fell apart, I was presented with the stark reality that it was a repeat of every relationship I had ever had. In the end, I was left with a huge mess of emotions—normal for how I'm wired— and a lot of confusion as to how it got to where it got.

In the beginning, of course, I blamed her. Why couldn't she just be who I wanted her to be? Then I blamed me: why couldn't I be different somehow and not have expectations or needs?

It took months to unravel the tangled memories of the experience. Months to understand that she is perfect the way she is and I'm perfect the way I am. Are we compatible? Hell no. Is that OK? Hell yes.

It took deep knowing of how we are programmed as humans to get there. Understanding that the combination of neurons and neurotransmitters with a long history of memories and stored opinions caused me to see things through a very specific lens.

Understanding deeply that we have little control over our thoughts and reactions was the door to freedom. Freedom from the interpretations that held me down.

What's the point of sharing this story? Once I was able to understand how we're all subject to the human condition, I was able to really get how perfect we both are in our own ways. I was able to lose the narrative of blame.

That narrative has been replaced by a deep love for me and for her, and a realization that we are both beautiful human beings. That's the power of accepting that we are biochemical machines with very specific programming.

In the end, what I'm left with, and what's available as a result, is a recognition that, although my programming is determined, awareness allows me to choose a direction for my thoughts. I can accept who we all are and move through the world with the ability to accept everyone right where they are, without reservation.

Powerful? Oh, you bet!

Now, the theme of this chapter is creation. Once you discern that we are the way we are and form an awareness of your programming, the path to creation is opened.

Creation occurs in the moment between your automatic responses and your choosing to recognize them, to be aware of them. In the moment of recognition, you get to choose to either go with the automatic, habituated responses or realize it for what it is and choose another direction.

Seeing human nature for what it is opens the door to freedom, allowing for overcoming, allowing for choice.

Ultimately, a way of living in the moment *opens up*, without any predetermined thought or action.

Think about it for a minute (obviously you'll think about a boatload of other things at the same time; it's how we're wired after all). And now, really think about what I'm about to say—you live into a future that's already predetermined by your past.

Take any example from your life. Let's say you go to a show. You go with an expectation that it will be a certain way. Where did that expectation come from? Another experience. Another emotion from the past. You hope this show will make you feel like the other show did. What happens? It could go either way—you could have a great night and say how much it was like that other great show you saw or it could be awful and you'll say how it didn't live up to your expectations (which is only a comparison to that great show from the past). Either way, you weren't really at the show, were you? Nope. You were living in the experience of the past show.

This concept can be applied to every experience. You are never truly in the moment. But, creation and new experiences happen with an awareness of the moment! Werner Erhard describes this as "living in the world of knowing" versus "living in the world of being" (Hyde and Kopp 2019).

We all live in the world of knowing, but very few of us live in the world of being; the true masters of life have perfected living in the world of being. However, knowing is not a bad thing. If I need brain surgery, it's comforting to me to know that my surgeon knows how to perform the surgery correctly. But that's not what I'm alluding to. Knowing is a great thing, but it's not where life is lived. Life is lived, life is created, in the present moment outside of your thoughts.

The awareness that I've been talking about, once internalized, creates the ability to really be present in the moment, to really be living life as it truly is, as it is meant to be experienced.

In a recent seminar on becoming a master of life, Landmark referred to this awareness as "living out in the nothing." At first I was perplexed about what that meant. They gave the example of being a child: when we're children, we explore the world with an enthusiastic and inquisitive nature, without any preconceived ideas about what the experience will be. That's what "living out in the nothing" is like—you are present in that moment, free to experience whatever the moment brings without deciding what the experience will be like in advance.

Can you see the possibilities? Can you see how magnificent life can be when connected to life moment to moment?

Anything is possible. Anything can be created from that point of view!

4

I Might as well be Me, Everyone Else is Taken

Because one believes in oneself, one doesn't try to
convince others. Because one is content with oneself,
one doesn't need others' approval. Because one accepts
oneself, the whole world accepts him or her.

Lao Tzu

In June of 1998 I was sitting at my desk with an empty, horrible feeling in my stomach. I had just been advised by Bank of America that they were exercising their option to close our line of credit, which had been run up to $300k over the preceding two years. Out of nowhere, no warning, no grace period. Just pay $300k in less than thirty days or we'll start liquidating. I had no idea how we were going to come up with the money, but the bank sure didn't give a damn how I did it; they were clear that it was going to happen, one way or another.

At that point in time everything on the outside looked great— we'd been running at a consistent $4MM annual revenue run rate, we'd made *Inc.* magazine's list of the 500 fastest growing companies in the US two years in a row, we had more than forty employees, and things looked great! Behind the scenes, we had little idea how to run a company. We responded to issues by hiring more people, which was the reason our line of credit had been extended.

If you've never been part of the process of forbearance (a fancy banking term for grabbing your scrotum in a vice and squeezing every penny out of you), then you've missed out on an opportunity to learn the truth about the banking industry. They charge you exorbitant monthly penalty fees for not shutting you down. Makes sense, right? They want their money; you have to continue to operate to get them their money, but in the meantime, they'll take every last penny and pretty much cut off your ability to increase revenue to meet the financial demands. Yay, bankers!

So here I was, sitting at the helm of a sinking ship, with no idea how to save it.

Was I stressed? Oh, you betcha! I had over forty employees relying on me to figure this out. It was all on me to determine our course of action.

My therapist at the time had recently been to Kripalu, a magnificent yoga retreat center located in the Berkshire mountains in Massachusetts. He suggested I take a week and attend a program designed to help you determine what your life is about and the what, where, and how of creating a new life. It couldn't have been more perfect.

Everyone around me called me crazy. How could I even think of disconnecting for a week, spending money I didn't have, and taking my eye off the ball.

I can say, without reservation, if I had not attended that weeklong session, my company would have failed, it would have been liquidated. The end.

What happened at Kripalu? What caused the shift in my thinking?

I was introduced to the idea that the way the world occurred for you was exactly how you thought it would. In other words, introspection, looking inside, and understanding what you are about was key to forming a new world view. I also learned that life was meant to be enjoyed—even in the so-called rough times. It's all just an amazing adventure, and stress is something we create with our thoughts about any particular situation.

When I returned from my week at Kripalu, I was a different person. I was calm, centered, and focused; the stress was gone!

In the end, the bank was paid their blood money within a year and a half. That company still thrives today, almost thirty-three years and counting, with my brother (my former partner) at the helm.

Here's my point, at long last: I had been looking outside myself for the answers as to how I was going to pay off the bank. I was looking for something external to fix the issue. Until I understood that all the answers had to do with me and my thoughts about it, I was stuck in that stress filled hell of a situation.

Once I had knowledge that I could enjoy the challenges of life, and I understood that the challenges were simply an opportunity to be creative, things shifted, and the solution was presented.

If the answers to any and all problems are centered right here inside of you, how do you uncover them? It goes back to chapters two and three. Using the tools described in these chapters creates the awareness we need to uncover the answers we're looking for.

To be clear, I'm not saying we don't look outside ourselves for the specific items required to solve an issue in our lives—I'm saying we start by looking inward and establishing the right frame of mind, the awareness to allow us to effectively and accurately determine the course of action required, and the tools that will make it all happen.

The right frame of mind is simply one of acceptance, joy, curiosity, and conviction.

Notice I use the word *simply*. They're truly simple concepts, but not easy apply to oneself. It's always that way—everything in our lives can be distilled down to simplicity. However, simplicity does not mean ease.

Weight loss is a concept most people can relate to. Weight loss is simple. Really, it is. You combine a certain regimen of diet and exercise, and viola, you lose weight. That being said, Why is it so hard for us to actually implement a weight loss regimen? Because it's simple, not easy. Seriously, it's not rocket science. It's as simple as 1+1=2. Do this and that will happen. It goes back to our biochemical nature. Figuring out what to eat, how much to eat, and when to eat it—it's not that hard! Why are there so many different diets? So many different companies offering the "easier" way to lose weight? Precisely because it's not easy.

If you look at acceptance as the first step in a powerful, positive frame of mind, do you accept where you are right now in regard to your weight? Probably not. But try that on for a minute: accept where you are as a result of how you've conducted your life so far. No guilt. No blame. Nothing to change. Just accept that you are whole, complete, and perfect exactly as you are right now. A simple concept—not easy in practice.

Again, try that on for a minute. What would it feel like simply to accept yourself, to accept your weight?

If you truly comprehend that where you are at in life is based on past experiences and genetics, you can accept your true self and be okay with who and where you are. This creates a strong foundation on which to begin choosing something different.

Joy! You can be joyful for who you are today. You can delight in every part of your amazing body. Think about it. There has never been another you. This is it. You are the best and only you there is. Be joyful about that! You can choose the easy path and focus on perceived flaws or you can accept and be joyful. Once you really grasp that you are the most amazing you there is, and you feel that joy coursing through you, things will naturally change!

Bring in curiosity. Curious people look at life as something to be explored, not judged. Not as a problem to be solved per se but as an opportunity to learn, to explore. Apply that to weight loss. Instead of feeling bad about carrying extra weight, be curious as to how you got here. Be curious as to why you stay here. Be curious as to how you eat, when you eat, what you eat. I'm talking about creating awareness. Curiosity allows you to bring a joyful, accepting attitude to whatever you're looking at. In this example it's weight loss, but you can apply it to any area of your life.

Finally, we arrive at conviction. Once we've accepted our current place without judgment or blame, once we've brought joy and curiosity into the mix, we're now ready for conviction. We're ready to commit to whatever new choice of action we'd like to take. In the case of weight loss, we're ready to commit ourselves with complete conviction to a new choice of eating differently and getting ourselves moving on a daily basis.

Notice that I haven't said what diet or what exercise routine you should follow? That's because . . . wait for it . . . they all work! Yes, they all work just as perfect as they are intended. We always think the latest diet or exercise regime is the one that works the best. Not so. We just want the softer, easier way, and we think the newest one is just that. Recognize that by bringing in the tools to create the right mind set, you can choose whatever diet you want, and weight loss will happen by sticking with it consistently. Conviction equals consistency.

Why is it so hard to accept ourselves as we are? A great deal has to do with the society we live in. Each and every day we're inundated with images and marketing messages that portray some ideal that doesn't exist except within the stories created by whoever wants to sell us something. Quite literally we're told time after time that something other than what we have will bring us the joy and happiness we're craving.

If only I could buy that new car. That beautiful waterfront home would solve all my problems. If I just sign up with the new weight loss company, I'll lose all this extra weight and feel good about me. Finally. Consider that this is all illusory. None of it matters. None of it matters. None of it will bring the joy you're looking for, and it's just that simple. All that stuff is just stuff. The you that is dissatisfied, that's not happy, that's longing for something will just be the same you in a new car or waterfront home. Things are not the answer. You are the answer.

Accepting you as you are. Accepting the things in your life exactly as they are will open up a new space for joy. Acceptance is the first step in manifesting the life you long for: one of joy and happiness. The "things" will naturally come along with that way of being, but you will have no attachment to them!

5

MOVE AND GROOVE
OR REST AND RUST

If you are in a bad mood go for a walk. If you are still in a
bad mood go for another walk.

Hippocrates

It was a cold, snowy afternoon as I limped slowly into the surgeon's office at New England Baptist Hospital. I was a week away from having invasive spinal surgery to repair two herniated discs that had been causing excruciating and debilitating sciatica (nerve pain) for the past two years. I'd injured my back twenty years earlier and it had gotten progressively worse over the years. I'd always been active, both in the gym and in general. I'd have occasional flare ups where I'd end up in the hospital emergency room for the standard injections of Toradol and steroids. That regimen worked for many years, but by 2014 I was in constant pain.

I'd been doing CrossFit for over a year at that time, and I pushed through the pain with some success.

Believe me, I had tried everything to heal my back.

I had enrolled in the spine program at New England Baptist hospital five years prior, and I had done everything they asked of me. I had had several rounds of cortisone shots (not the most pleasant experience for someone who hates needles!). Nothing seemed to work, and by mid-2014 I'd been referred for surgery. When I say I was in pain, I mean I was in pain every single moment of every single day.

The week before the scheduled date, I called my surgeon to say that I felt just a little bit better, the pain had subsided to the point I finally had a good night's sleep, and I was back at the gym. I asked for his opinion: should I continue at the gym, put off surgery, and see how it goes or get the surgery over with and start the recovery process?

His *exact* words were: "I don't want to see you until you're dragging your ass across the rug in my waiting room."

I took his advice, and at that moment I committed myself to getting into the gym again with the focused goal of increasing my core strength. Fast forward to today, I've had no back flare ups since that time! Working out, specifically CrossFit, has increased my core strength, stabilized my spine, and given me an opportunity to resume any and all activities with little pain. Don't get me wrong, I still have back pain and stiffness from time to time, but nothing like it was; it's normal back pain associated with daily living and, well, aging.

The point of the story is getting active and committing to a regular exercise routine saved me from surgery that may or may not have had a positive outcome.

The second leading cause of preventable death in the United States, behind tobacco use, is a sedentary lifestyle. Think about that. People are literally dying from something they could easily fix—sitting around and not moving their bodies and not eating the right foods (we'll talk about food in the next chapter). That is so sad! It's easy to get into the habit of not moving. It takes effort to get up and get moving, and it's even more difficult to keep it going.

Think of the gym the week after New Year's Day. Filled to the brim with people committed to getting healthy. Fast forward to a scant thirty days later—a virtual ghost town. What happened? Habits, baby. As we discovered earlier, we're all creatures of habit. Good or bad— your mind doesn't care. Habits are hardwired in our brains, and so by the end of the first month, we've already slipped back into our old routine. Pushing past that first thirty-day mark is simple but not easy. It takes awareness, which you've learned is the key to guiding your habits.

What's the best form of exercise? Same as the best form of meditation—the one you do consistently! Whether it's CrossFit, weightlifting, tai chi, yoga, Pilates, barre, or some other exercise, the most important thing is consistency. Whatever resonates with you where you are in your life.

I've been working out since USMC bootcamp, in 1979, at the tender age of seventeen. Prior to bootcamp, I was not physically active, unless smoking and drinking are considered physical activity! It was so bad that my drill instructors threatened to ship me off to the "pork chop" platoon. As you can imagine, it's not the platoon for physically fit individuals. Luckily that experience instilled in me the idea that you need to move every single day to be physically ready to tackle any challenge.

Over the years I've done it all. Weightlifting, bodybuilding, step aerobics, high and low impact aerobics, body sculpting, racquetball, yoga, tai chi, kickboxing, running, and now CrossFit. I've tried them all, and each has been extremely effective and enjoyable in its own unique way.

The bottom line is consistency. That's the key to maintaining a healthy body. Pick something, anything, and be consistent. It goes back to the idea: you come first. You are the most important person in your life, and dedicating time to physical activity benefits everyone else around you.

What are the benefits of regular exercise?

Exercise Controls Weight

Besides looking better (if that's your goal), decreasing weight takes strain and stress off your body. Every system in your body benefits from decreased weight—your joints, your heart, your hormonal system—all of them benefit from not having to support the additional body mass. Combining exercise and better nutrition, without a doubt, decreases overall weight.

Exercise Combats Health Conditions and Diseases

Diabetes

Type II diabetes, also known as adult onset diabetes, is in most cases related to poor nutritional choices and a sedentary lifestyle. Many people avoid the awful consequences of this disease by simply introducing exercise into their lives. Regular exercise leads to weight loss which, in turn, allows for better management of blood glucose and insulin resistance—both related to diabetes.

Metabolic Syndrome

Metabolic Syndrome is the combination of related cardiovascular risk factors: insulin resistance, elevated fasting blood sugar, hypertension, elevated triglycerides, low HDL cholesterol, and abdominal obesity. It's estimated over 40 percent of Americans are affected by this syndrome. The common factor here is increased weight—it induces all of these risk factors. Lose weight, and these risk factors, for the most part, go away. Don't exercise, and these factors eventually lead to diabetes. Honestly, I think people don't know how devastating diabetes is. My father's mother was diabetic, as was her father. Her father lost both legs and an eye to diabetes. My grandmother suffered several strokes over her lifespan. Two of my siblings have diabetes. None of them exercised with any consistency.

Arthritis

Arthritis affects about 1 in 4 people. Exercise, combined with other healthy lifestyle choices, can help combat this condition. Movement, when possible, is great for increasing mobility and decreasing inflammation.

Falls

For older folks this is an important point. As we age, we lose muscle mass and we lose our balance more easily. We also lose mobility. All these lead to the likelihood we'll experience a fall. How many elderly friends or family do you know who suffered a fall, broke a hip, and that was it—the end. Exercise decreases the negative aspects of aging and helps us maintain our independence.

Hypertension

Regular exercise can decrease blood pressure. Weight loss or consistent cardio conditioning exercise can help reduce your blood pressure.

Back Issues

Almost everyone will experience back pain at some point in their lives. Let's face it—we're not meant to stand upright. But here we are. As I talked about earlier, I was a week away from major spine surgery, however, a recommitment to regular exercise allowed me to avoid that risky surgery. Core strength exercises stabilize your entire abdominal and spinal region. By strengthening my core, my lower back is supported, my vertebrae move out of place less often, and it decreased the irritation of the nerves in that area, which in turn has decreased or eliminated my back pain! Squats, squats, squats is my mantra!

Exercise Improves Mood

For me, this one is literally life or death. Treating my medication-resistant depression requires that I exercise regularly: my mood is directly tied to exercise. If I maintain a regular exercise program, it's guaranteed that my mood will be positive and healthy. If I slip out of my routine, it's not long before the negative thoughts pop up, and then I'm on my way to a place I don't want to go.

It's that simple—exercise good, no exercise bad. The year 2018 was a case in point. My whole life, by choice, was upended. I moved to New York City, I was in a situation where I was busy working 24/7, and I willingly changed my routine of regular exercise. By the end of the summer, my depression had returned with a vengeance and wreaked havoc in my life. Since October 2018 I've been back in a regular routine of working out, and my depression is gone. It's just that simple.

Exercise Boosts Energy

I'm known in my circle of friends as the guy to ask for last minute adventures. I'm the yes-man. I say yes to just about everything that comes along, and I love it! But that means I need to have available energy for the long days and fun-filled nights. Exercise provides that energy.

Exercise Promotes Better Sleep

Sleep is underrated. You can go without food for a long while, without water for a bit, but if you go without sleep, you quickly begin the descent toward death. It's that important! Sleep is where all the repair happens. It's the regeneration time for your body. I work with a lot of people who want to sleep better. We use cannabis as a healthy means to create better sleep, but I also strongly advise getting enough exercise. Exercise is key to good sleep. Try it, you be the judge.

Exercise Puts the Spark Back in Your Sex Life

Who doesn't like good sex or bad sex, or for that matter, any sex! A healthy sex life provides amazing benefits by itself. Exercise makes you feel better, makes you feel more attractive, and increases your stamina. But there's even more to it than that. Regular physical activity may enhance arousal for women, and men who exercise regularly are less likely to have problems with erectile dysfunction than men who don't exercise. If this isn't enough to get you out there and exercising, then we have a lot more work to do!

Exercise Can Be Fun and Social

I am, beyond the shadow of a doubt, a social creature. I love people. I love interacting with them. I've always loved group classes: yoga, aerobics, tai chi, any and all group classes. That's one of the things I enjoy most about CrossFit. The community aspect of CrossFit has been studied at Harvard University; researchers looked at why and how we gather together as social animals. Without a doubt we are social creatures, and exercising together, in whatever modality you choose, will reap benefits galore.

CrossFit & HIIT

Here's the part where I get up on my soapbox and expound upon the reasons why I think CrossFit, or any high intensity interval training (HIIT), is the best form of exercise, hands down.

I am, without a doubt, in the best physical shape of my life at the age of fifty-seven. As I mentioned before, I've been at this for forty years now, and I have done every modality of exercise possible. My current level of fitness, which I believe is higher than any other point in time, I owe to CrossFit. Without the regular high intensity of CrossFit, I'd be in a far different place.

The basic premise of HIIT is simple: exercise at a high intensity for alternating short periods of time. My experiences have shown that HIIT is the best format out there for creating muscle mass and increasing stamina; there isn't a better overall body workout than a HIIT format like CrossFit. Does it sound like I drank the cool aid?

Yep, but I also know stuff. I'm trained in healthcare. I see what happens when you don't exercise.

I'm going to talk to my peers now—you younger folks can hold on, or even better, listen in because you're going to be here sooner than you think.

Folks, shit happens as you age. I'm sure you're feeling it already if you're over the age of fifty. You're going to continue to lose muscle mass. This is not a little thing! Everything will be affected as this happens: everything from how you store fat to how you metabolize drugs.

Let's start with your balance. Have you experienced it yet? That moment when you take that leap you've done a million times in the past and suddenly you're not so sure you're going to land well.

I've noticed it: walking up the bleachers at a sporting event or jumping off the dock onto the boat. Something is different; I'm not as steady as I once was.

It's coming and you have to be ready.

HIIT. Get in there—start moving.

A misconception I hear all the time is that if you do CrossFit, you'll get injured. Well, you can be injured doing anything. I can't tell you the number of times I hear the silliest stories about how someone got injured. Everything from "my dog yanked me over" to "I slipped in the shower." Let me tell you: after seven years of doing this particular form of exercise, I can say, without a doubt, you will decrease your chances of unexpected injury by doing CrossFit. One note of interest—in December 2019 CrossFit won a four million dollar lawsuit against the National Strength and Conditioning Association for fraudulently publishing data that was designed to create the illusion that CrossFit caused more injuries than other modes of exercise. The studies cited by the NSCA were proven to be patently false, and the lead researcher was forced to resign his position at a prestigious university as a result of these falsifications (crossfit.com 2019). Don't believe everything you hear!

It's simple really—by working ALL of your body using functional movements, you'll increase your overall fitness level.

What do I mean by functional movements?

One of the foundations of CrossFit is just that—functional movement. All of the exercises, whether for conditioning or strength training, are based on movements that come naturally to your body. You know, movements you use every day, like squatting down to pick up your kid or grandkid or lifting something overhead to put it up on a shelf. Doing basic resistance movements increases your overall fitness and prepares you to participate fully in everyday life activities!

Another common objection I hear is "it's too strenuous for me." Isn't that the point? Are you so out of shape you can't do a bit of strenuous work? That's the beauty of CrossFit—the workouts never last more than sixty minutes. Boom, and you're done. But, even better, you can scale to your ability any workout. Do you really think that at the age of fifty-seven I'm going head to head with twenty-five-year-old studs? Hell no. I scale my workouts to match what my current level of fitness is and current level of abilities. Again, that's the joy of CrossFit!

Since we've been talking about things brain related in earlier chapters why stop now. Crossfit (HIIT) stimulates production of BDNF, brain derived neurotrophic factor, which is a critical component of a healthy brain. BDNF has been shown to be instrumental in the creation of new neurons as well as glucose homeostasis and lipid metabolization. (Jimenez-Maldonado et al. 2018)

When looking for a CrossFit gym, beware not all gyms are created equal. There is a movement in the CrossFit gym community to more inclusive programming. Standard CrossFit programming is not easy by any stretch of the imagination and many gyms are weaving in alternative programming that creates a fantastic workout using varying modalities. I travel a lot and drop in to many different gyms. My home gym, Vagabond CrossFit, has *the* best programming. Kevin O'Malley, the owner, combines CrossFit movements with other variations to create an extremely effective program. Check it out at www.vagabondcrossfit.com. My point is this, try out a few gyms until you find one that fits.

Yoga

Remember I said earlier that I've done a lot of stuff in my life? I wasn't kidding!

As I mentioned in a previous chapter, I had attended a yoga/meditation retreat back in 1998 as a result of a recommendation from my therapist. At that point, I was about as stressed as a person could be, and I was at the breaking point.

That week changed my life. It very literally changed the course of the next twenty years. You have to remember that this was at the very beginning of the yoga boom in the United States. It was still a relatively small group of people practicing on a regular basis. I was enamored with yoga. When I say yoga relieved all my stress, I mean I went from ten to one on the stress scale.

If it isn't apparent yet, I'm wired to go all in when I like something. That's just what I did with yoga. When I returned from my weeklong transformation, I immediately enrolled in the only local yoga studio in town, which was owned and operated by one of the most lovely, caring people I've had the pleasure to know, Maria Baldwin.

Maria had just completed her doctorate in education and quickly became my mentor and instructor. She had just completed creating the first curriculum for a yoga teacher certification, and I immersed myself. After graduation, I became a teacher and avid student of all things yoga and meditation. Talk about a transformation!

Since that time, I have attended numerous workshops on the benefits of yoga. One of the most impactful was a weeklong training called Science of Yoga for Healthcare Professionals, presented at Kripalu Center for Yoga & Health.

I spent the week alongside like-minded physicians, nurses, and other healthcare providers, learning about the rigorous, evidence-based scientific studies that conclusively prove the myriad of benefits of yoga. Kripalu has been aligned with many of the world-class higher education institutions for years, directly studying the effects of yoga and meditation.

I feel like we need to clear something up here. I keep mentioning yoga and meditation together as if they are one. In fact, they can be considered one in the same or as separate entities altogether. It comes down to your personal viewpoint.

For a lot of people, yoga is another form of exercise or stretching. For others, like me, it's a form of meditation that includes postures and movements. It doesn't matter which way you come at it—if you practice, you will benefit.

One of the things I used to hear a lot when talking about yoga (and meditation) with people was "I just can't sit still that long." When I heard that, it made me think, "Well then you need this more than anybody then, don't you?" Seriously, if someone believes they can't focus attention that long on something so beneficial, I can only imagine what the rest of their life looks like; I think it's commonly called a "shit show."

To my point, if you want to reign in the shit show, start doing yoga and meditate.

So, nurseMARK, what are the positive benefits of yoga? I'm glad you asked that question! Lisa Nelson and Angela Wilson, developers of the Science of Yoga for Healthcare Professionals course, describe the following benefits:

Musculoskeletal disorders

Improved:

- Flexibility
- Balance
- Spinal movement
- Pain tolerance

Decreased:

- Fall risk
- Use of pain medication

- Disability

Neurologic disorders

- Decreased seizure frequency
- Lessens chronic pain
- Increased mobility and decreased fall risk in Parkinson's disease

Cardiovascular disorders

- Lower systolic and diastolic blood pressure
- Fewer episodes of angina
- Improved exercise tolerance in CHF

Metabolic disorders

- Improved cholesterol profiles
- Lower BMI

Pregnancy

- Decreased back and leg pain
- Decreased labor pain

Mental Health

Improved outcomes for:

- Depression
- Anxiety
- PTSD
- Substance dependence
- Stress

- Eating disorders

Increases:

- Well-being
- Self-acceptance
- Body acceptance
- Emotional regulation

I don't know about you but that list just blows my mind! And that's only what we've been able to document and study. I'm certain the list has grown since this was published.

The bottom line is this: if you want to create a life you love, you have to be healthy physically and mentally. Yoga (and meditation) are only going to help make that a reality!

Tai Chi and Other Modalities

By now you can see I'm passionate about exercise and movement as being part and parcel to creating a life you love. There are so many other forms of movement that are effective. Here are some others I love:

Tai-Chi. This ancient Chinese form of martial arts has morphed into a practice used by millions to enhance longevity and health. It's focus on slow, controlled movements creates an opportunity for meditation in motion. In fact, it might be just the thing for you people who believe "I couldn't possibly sit still long enough for meditation." Here ya go! This is right up your alley! You get to move *and* meditate. I like the fact that you can practice this at any age—the older the better.

For the older crowd, the benefits to increased stability and balance are powerful.

Pilates. Pilates is a form of controlled exercise that originated in the early twentieth century. There is a focus on core strength, and for that reason I love it! Creating a strong core is key to maintaining a healthy back, allowing for full participation in life.

There are so many others: barre, spin, boxing, kickboxing, running, etc. The most important thing to remember is to simply pick something that you enjoy and stick with it.

Let's bring it back around now—back to the key—to awareness. Being aware of your body, being aware of how you treat it with exercise.

Ready, set, go!!!!

6

You Are What You Eat

Let food be your medicine, let medicine be your food

Ancient Greek Medicine

When I was in junior high school it seemed that everyone but me had a girlfriend. I was a chubby kid, not that attractive, and both my best friends had girlfriend's way before I ever did. I'd always been a little overweight, not awful but enough for my friends to tease me.

I can still remember being twelve years old and being taunted for wearing a brand of pants marketed by Sears called "Husky." HUSKY! What fucking marketing genius thought it would be good to put that label on portly adolescents? Nice, real nice. No wonder Sears has disappeared. Good riddance.

It's funny how that sets you up for a lasting body image. Even at my best I still look in the mirror and see a fat kid who couldn't find a date if his life depended on it. That's why I now consider myself somewhat of an expert on dieting. I've tried them all and I mean all.

Let's do a quick review of some of the lovely diets I've enjoyed:

- The Cabbage Soup Diet

- Body for Life
- Hollywood Diet
- Kraft Macaroni & Cheese and dry tuna diet (I made that one up myself!)
- Weight Watchers
- Atkins
- South Beach Diet
- Zone Diet
- Paleolithic diet
- Ketogenic diet
- intermittent fasting

There were others for sure, but these were the ones I really committed to.

What did they all have in common? I stopped doing them all at some point.

It goes back a couple of chapters to the great "habitualizer." You know, that part of your brain that notices what you do more than once and makes it a habit? Yeah, that thing.

It gets even worse. When it comes to food, a whole lot of other factors come into play. We literally have emotional connections to what we eat. I'll give you an example.

My family is known for cooking comfort foods. Things high in carbohydrates and low in fiber. Where it comes from, I don't know, but it's multigenerational. Now I'm not saying I don't love comfort foods, but I know they are not healthy choices.

Try to stop me if someone makes spaghetti with meat sauce. Go ahead, I dare you. You're taking your life in your hands there, bub. I can, and have, eaten pounds of spaghetti myself in one sitting. OK, perhaps that's why I was a bit overweight as a kid.

My point is I know it's not a good choice, I know its carb overload, I know physiologically what happens when it's converted in my body. Knowing makes no difference, and I've known it for a very long time! It was habit for us to have that meal once a week.

I've been able to establish a new habit of not having that pound of spaghetti, but that means I had to create a new habit of not making that meal. Here's the thing with habits that you may not know—you never get rid of the old habit, especially with food; it's there, etched in your memory just waiting for it to be put back in play. You install the new habit over the old one. That new habit becomes the well-worn pathway that chooses for you. But it takes one slip and you just might find yourself making pasta every Tuesday night again!

I use the example of cigarette smoking to illustrate my point. I smoked for years. After eating, after sex, while drinking alcohol, with my coffee: you get the idea. It was ingrained in everything I did. Of course, nicotine made sure I'd continue by virtue of that dopamine bump every time I lit up. The most difficult part of quitting, and I quit many, many times, was changing those habits and installing new ones. Why did I go back to smoking after quitting so many times? Because the old habits were still there in my neuronal connections. They were still there in my brain, just sitting there waiting to be used. Let's recognize how awesome that actually is—even though in this example it's smoking, think about how awesome our brain is to keeps habits on file in case we need to use them. I'm sure that came in handy back in the day when you had other things to contend with, like tigers eating you for breakfast.

Now, consider that eating is far more powerful than smoking (or any other drug). We have to eat. We can't simply stop doing it and do something else instead. Couple that with all those emotions and habits and you can see how much more difficult it is to change eating habits. Even more—once you recognize that foods really act like drugs, you can get the enormity of the issue!

Science is now showing us that foods do, in fact, act like drugs in the body. Let's take sugar for example. Lovely, tasty, yummy sugar. This little gem has been around for centuries. If you think about it, sugar played a large role in the expansion of civilization. The discovery and expansion of the new world was supported by sugar production. Slavery was part and parcel to that. The sugar cane production in the Caribbean and South America fueled slavery and, with it, the economy of the time.

Imagine all that power in one little plant. Why? Because it's like any other drug—it feels good to use it. Our bodies respond to it. Ingesting it kicks off that dopamine rush, and we're reinforced to do it again over and over. Honestly folks, it's a simple closed loop system that keeps us doing something that we all now know, really know, is bad for us as human organisms.

Its tradition to follow a meal with something sweet. But do we have to do that? Really?

Of course, we don't.

The statistics are in, over 60 percent of Americans are overweight. You see it. You know it. Do you think these folks don't know that what their eating and drinking is causing the problem? They know.

They know and they can't stop. Because . . . it's like any other drug—addictive and difficult to stop.

The medical care costs of obesity in the United States are high. In 2008 dollars, these costs were estimated to be $147 billion. The annual nationwide loss of production costs of obesity-related absenteeism range between $3.38 billion ($79 per obese individual) and $6.38 billion ($132 per obese individual) (Centers for Disease Control and Prevention).

It's more than the cost of care—consider the impact on the person and their loved ones.

In the US we're presented with a myriad of food selections. The easiest foods to acquire and least expensive also happen to be the worst for us. Think fast food here. Do you want to supersize that? Do you realize that was a genius sales and marketing ploy which also contributed to the obesity epidemic? For a scant one dollar more, you can have double the sugary drink and processed foods, which are noxious to your health. Yay, fast food!

The obesity epidemic is a perfect example of human nature. Knowing is nothing without action. The old adage "knowledge is power" is bullshit. The truth is that knowledge is power only when put into action. Everyone knows what the deal is and still we have this issue.

Why did I bring this up? You may or may not have an issue with weight, but nutrition, what you eat, when you eat it, and how much you eat, all play into how your magnificent, amazing human machine is going to run.

Let me share some of my experience here about what has worked and has not worked for me.

First and foremost, dieting is bullshit. Plain and simple. You know it. I know it. Let's not continue the fantasy.

Don't get me wrong, dieting will cause you to lose weight . . . and you'll gain it back again (and sometimes more) when you can't sustain the discipline of whatever diet you've selected. Trust me, I've been there.

Case in point—I have more than one friend who went so far as to have major gastric bypass surgery in an attempt to lose weight only to gain that weight back within a year. Why? Food is a drug, plain and simple. They didn't change their brain wiring; they only changed the physical aspect of eating, not the more important mental aspect.

My experience is this: the best diet is the one you can stick with most of the time. Now to be clear, my definition of diet moving forward in this chapter refers to what we eat on a regular basis, the accumulation of everything we put in our bodies, not a reference to draconian fad diets designed to merely cause weight loss.

Let's all agree that there are as many opinions about a healthy diet as there are people. Then consider that each individual is a unique chemical equation. You can see how blanket recommendations might not be adequate when talking health and nutrition!

I'm seeing a trend in America (maybe it's just the circles I operate in): there is a move toward a more plant-based diet. And not only plants but organic, pesticide free plants. With mounting evidence showing a wide variety of health issues (cancer immediately comes to mind) being related to pesticide use, it's no wonder folks are looking for more healthy alternatives.

Almost every single diet I've been on that was worth its weight had vegetables as a key component. I mean every single one. Seems to me that says something about the power of vegetables in our diet. Some had very specific vegetables that you could eat, and others said eat all you want of whatever veggies you want.

What is it about vegetables that make them so good for you? Well, how much time do you have? I could go on for a long time talking about the virtues of vegetables in our diet: vegetables are a great source of fiber which aides in digestion; they contain vitamins and nutrients that sustain life; and many vegetables also contain antioxidants which, if you haven't heard, are beneficial in warding off inflammation, aging, and cancer. Veggies are so good there are a large number of people who only eat vegetables. Every day I see more folks moving in that direction for a number of reasons, the least of which is it's super healthy!

The bottom line is, eat vegetables.

Veggies good; very, very good.

Similar to vegetables, fruits offer many of the same benefits as they're plant brethren. A healthy dose of fruit can keep you fit and trim. Plus, fruit tastes good! You want to satisfy that sweet tooth? Instead of having that cupcake, reach for some fruit. You'll be just as satisfied and much healthier in the end.

On to protein! Meat, meat, and more meat. As mentioned earlier there is a move to eat less meat in our diets and more fruits and vegetables. As also mentioned earlier, our relationship to food is complex.

For me, being of Scottish and English descent, meat and fish are staples of my diet. I mean we eat every part of the animal. Ever heard of haggis? The Scots are known to be frugal, and this is a perfect example. Basically, haggis is every internal part of the sheep that the butcher wouldn't buy stuffed into the stomach and boiled. Mm, waste not want not I always say.

Meat. I love meat. I love fish.

There are battle lines drawn over whether meat is healthy or not healthy. The old adage "everything in moderation" is important to keep in mind here. We'll talk further about this in a bit when we talk KETO.

Veggies, Fruits, Meats. Those are the top three for me. What about grains and dairy?

I grew up on the standard American diet of dairy and grains. Breakfast, lunch, and dinner included something from these two groups. A tall glass of milk and a grilled cheese sandwich—could there be a better lunch? These days, however, I limit my intake of both of these.

Why the change? I realized that dairy products were really well marketed and probably not what humans were originally supposed to be consuming. I can't imagine anyone back in antiquity latching onto a cow's udder for a little top off! So I slowly weaned myself off milk.

What about butter? Well, we were told butter and whole milk is bad for us. Remember that? That dietary advice from the government coincided with the rise in obesity. Are they connected? Who knows? I didn't use butter for years, and when I did drink milk, it was skim only.

What about grains? Delicious, wonderful bread. Oh, how I love fresh baked bread or hot rolls with dinner. Do I eat them? From time to time. But as a rule, I avoid grains. Luckily you see a lot of gluten free options in the marketplace today. There are some experts who believe grains contribute to leaky gut syndrome. The thought is that the gut, which is designed to contain all toxins, develops leaks that allow toxins to infiltrate the abdominal cavity and wreak havoc throughout.

Tracking

Tracking what you eat is crucial for successfully changing and sticking to your diet.

The first thing I do when coaching people on health and wellness is have them download either Lose It! or MyFitnessPal. Both of these apps are wonderful tools to track what you eat. Both provide the option to create specific measurement formats. By formats I mean setting up the tracking of macronutrients (i.e., carbs, proteins, and fats). This is key when you're trying to dial in a specific diet like Paleo or Keto.

Until you can quantify what you eat every day, you really have no base to start from. In order to be successful you need to have that data! It's all about clearly seeing what you're doing, and from that you can identify certain patterns of action. Once you gain that knowledge, you can put it into action and increase the likelihood you'll reach your goals.

It's tough at first to remember to track every meal, but after a week or so, it actually becomes fun to see what's really happening with your relationship to food.

It just occurred to me that before we get to the specific diets, I should also get into the weight measurement versus body fat measurement discussion.

In the midnineties during a routine physical I noticed my doctor writing the word *obese* in my chart: I exclaimed, "whoa now, what the fuck is that all about?!" Those were my exact words (my doc and I are close). He explained that according to the Body Mass Index (BMI) chart, I was obese. Boy, did that piss me off. I was far from what I consider obese. I was pretty damn buff at that point in time.

Here's the problem with the BMI—it doesn't distinguish between fat and muscle. Muscle and fat take up different amounts of mass in the body. In effect the BMI is an inaccurate measurement of obesity.

That's why I believe weight loss is not the goal. Instead, achieving a healthy body fat percentage is much more accurate and desired.

You can have your body fat percentage measured at any quality gym, and most of the electronic home scales today have that feature. In any event, stop looking at your weight and look at your body fat percentage. You'll be happy when you see the results.

7

WHAT'S NEW IS WHAT'S OLD: CURRENT DIETARY TRENDS

Don't dig your grave with your own knife and fork.

Old English Proverb

In this chapter we'll cover four of the top diet-related trends in eating and a healthy lifestyle. Let's get to it!

The top four dietary trends today, in my mind, are the Paleolithic diet, Zone Diet, ketogenic diet, and intermittent fasting. All four have been around in some form or another, for many years, and have science to back them up.

The Paleolithic Diet

Let's start with Paleo, which is commonly referred to as the caveman diet. This was the first "darling" of the CrossFit movement. Everyone used the Paleo diet, and a lot of CrossFitters still do. As the name suggests, the diet is based on what folks believe our ancestors ate back in the days we lived in caves; this would have been prior to the advent of subsistence farming and modern livestock cultivation. This diet leans heavily on meats, vegetables, and fruits, and it excludes all processed foods and dairy. Why dairy? The thought is that cows were not domesticated until after the Paleolithic period.

Paleo is a commitment for sure! You really have to be prepared to cook most of your meals or sign on with a meal plan service. You do, over time, learn how to negotiate a restaurant menu, but if you're really focused on this particular diet, you'll be cooking a lot. That's actually a good thing—there is something very satisfying about cooking for yourself or others, so there's that added benefit!

Pros: clean diet, more energy, less food related allergies, and fat loss. Cons: the food preparation and cooking can be overwhelming.

The Zone Diet

Next up is one of my favorite diets: the Zone Diet. The Zone Diet was outlined in the bestselling book published in 1995 by Dr. Barry Sears. The main premise of the Zone Diet is insulin regulation. By eating a combination of foods, you can regulate your insulin levels and achieve optimum health. Here are a few of the reported positive benefits of adopting the Zone Diet (Sears and Lawren 1995):

- Permanent loss of excess body fat
- Dramatic reduction in the risk of chronic diseases, such as heart disease, diabetes, and cancer
- Improved mental and physical performance
- A longer life

"The Zone" is the state of optimum health achieved by using this recommended diet.

I love that the Zone Diet is based on science. Being a nurse, and a bit of a closet nerd, I love a good science-based approach to eating, and the Zone Diet is just that.

A lot of attention is paid to the *glycemic load* of the foods you consume. The glycemic load refers to the calculation of the density of the carbohydrate and the rate it enters the bloodstream. Yay, science!

Typically, all vegetables and fruits are acceptable, but there are exceptions. For instance, corn, carrots, and all of the starchy vegetables are high on the glycemic index and not encouraged in The Zone Diet. As well as bananas and raisins from the fruit side of the house. Everything else is allowed in moderation.

The reason these guidelines for glycemic load are in place is that the higher the glycemic load the more it will affect insulin levels.

Moderation is the key word for the Zone Diet. Combining low-fat protein with an equal amount of low glycemic load vegetables is optimum.

The last item to add to the plate is fat. Fat has been maligned for many years, with dire results. The lack of good fats in the American diet has contributed to the high rate of obesity. The low-fat, or no fat, diets recommended by the government have been disastrous.

Not all fats are good, but good fats are good. Science has shown us that fat is required for optimum health. Eating the right amount of fats is imperative to maintaining good health. Fats are normally categorized in the following way: saturated, unsaturated, and trans. By now you've heard trans fats are bad for you. Go figure that a man-made, processed fat would be bad for you. Time and time again we're finding out that the food nature provides is perfect exactly as it is.

When it's adulterated to make it less expensive to produce, we run into trouble.

Saturated fats, typically hard at room temps (think coconut oil), have had a bad rap for a long while. Low and behold, we've now determined that perhaps the experts were wrong, and we need some saturated fats in our diet.

Unsaturated fats come in two forms: monounsaturated and polyunsaturated. It's simple chemistry really—it has to do with the amount of double bonds present in its chemical makeup.

> Monounsaturated fats are made up of a chain of carbon with one pair of carbon molecules joined by a double bond. The more double bonds there are, the more solid the fat will be. Monounsaturated fats are generally liquid at room temperature, but turn slightly solid when chilled. Polyunsaturated fats have two or more double bonds between carbon atoms in the carbon chain backbone of the fat. They are more solid than monounsaturated fats but less so than saturated fats. This makes polyunsaturated fats also liquid at room temperature (Coila 2018).

Monounsaturated fats are liquid at room temperature and are typically found in the following foods:

- Olive oil
- Canola oil
- Peanut oil
- Nuts
- Avocados

We've all heard about the benefits of two kinds of polyunsaturated fats: Omega-3 and Omega-6. In the typical American diet we consume far too many Omega-6 fatty acids and not enough Omega-3 fatty acids. Omega-3 is most prevalent in fish oil, especially in cold water fishes. Omega-6 is found in a lot of common foods: chicken, sausage, hot dogs, chips—you know, the four main food groups. Ha!

These fats are critical to maintaining a healthy body. As you'll see in the next part of this chapter, fats can be a main source of energy as well.

Pros: science-based approach, balanced across all food sources (meat, vegetables, fruits), lots of variety in the diet. Cons: the Zone Diet can be confusing; there is a bit of a learning curve.

The Ketogenic Diet

Now to the newest kid on the block. Well, not really the newest, more a renewal of an oldie but goodie. The ketogenic diet is based on maintaining a diet that forces the body to go into a state called *ketosis*. In actuality, you're forcing your body, through a specific process, to change from burning carbohydrates for energy to burning stored fat. It's a neat evolutionary trick left over from the days when starvation was a real issue.

Your body has this amazing process whereby, if you aren't able to ingest enough carbohydrates, it alerts the liver to begin breaking down fats for energy. This process produces ketones, which take the place of glucose (the fuel from digesting and metabolizing carbohydrates) as fuel for the brain and the body. You find out if you've successfully pushed your body into ketosis by testing your urine for the presence of ketones.

This diet is a high fat, adequate protein, low-carbohydrate diet.

One little known fact—this diet has been around since the 1920s, and it was the primary dietary treatment for childhood epilepsy. Keto is still in use today as a treatment for epilepsy, and it has been studied and documented for years. And you still don't think foods are drugs? C'mon! Really?

When I began my keto period, I was no stranger to implementing a diet. I'd had plenty of experience with all those crazy fads in the past, but my experience with the Paleo and Zone diets made it easy for me to implement keto.

So, what kinds of things can you eat on keto? Here are the top fifteen foods typically included in a keto diet:

- **Seafood.** Hailing from New England, I love and eat plenty of seafood.
- **Low-carb veggies.** No starchy veggies (potatoes, carrots, corn, peas)—they'll push you over your carb limit with one serving.
- **Cheese.** Mm cheese.
- **Avocados.** Chock full of potassium, which might help transition to keto.
- **Meat and Poultry.** Last time I checked, chickens were made of meat!
- **Eggs.** I love eggs. Seriously, they are like the perfect food. Easy to cook, easy to carry.
- **Coconut Oil.** Made up of MCT (medium chain triglycerides) oils, which are converted immediately by the liver—fast and simple.
- **Plain Greek Yogurt and Cottage Cheese.**

- **Olive Oil.** You know this is good for you right? Have you heard of the Mediterranean diet? It includes lots of olive oil.
- **Nuts and seeds.** Who doesn't love nuts? Peanuts, by the way, are not nuts. Shocking right? Yep. They're legumes.
- **Berries.** Most fruits are too high-carb for the keto diet, but not berries!
- **Butter and Cream.** I know, me too. I bought into the bullshit story these were bad. But if my grandparents were any indication, they lived well into their 80s with all their food slathered in butter. My grandmother even put butter on the bread for peanut butter and jelly sandwiches. I have a long love affair with butter (I may have a butter problem).
- **Olives.** Ah, olives again. First olive oil, and now right to the source. Yay, olives!
- **Unsweetened Coffee and Tea.** No, not a vanilla chai latte! *Unsweetened* coffee and tea.
- **Dark Chocolate and Cocoa Powder.** Do I really need to say anything else? They're good—eat them.

I was concerned at first about the lack of carbs, to be honest. Doing CrossFit three to four times a week is strenuous, and I was concerned about the loss of energy. On keto, I was pleasantly surprised to find I had plenty of energy throughout the workout and throughout my day.

Due to its huge popularity at the moment, there are a multitude of places to go for information on what you can eat. Literally type in keto diet, and you'll be inundated with options. Don't be fooled into paying for anything; download an app you can use to track your keto diet.

Pros: delicious if you are a meat and cheese lover, easy to figure out and maintain.

Cons: not sure it's a long-term menu—the nurse in me says it's great to achieve a weight loss goal, but keto is not a diet you follow forever; it gets boring!

Intermittent Fasting

Intermittent fasting is a hot topic these days. As part of the Isagenix program, a meal replacement and supplement company, you fast one to two days a week. You're encouraged to use their chocolate snacks and proprietary drinks to have *some* nourishment. I liked it. It was a nice break from eating. Did I see results? Yes!

Intermittent fasting, for most folks today, takes the form of fasting sixteen hours and eating during an eight-hour window (16:8). The premise is that your body, if given enough time in between eating and abstinence, will naturally start burning fat for energy rather than converting carbs from what you eat.

Here are some proposed benefits to intermittent fasting:

- Decreased risk of obesity and metabolic disease
- Lower blood glucose levels
- Lower body fat storage
- Increased production of human growth hormone (we manufacture less in our bodies as we age, hence the lower energy level)
- Retraining of the hunger hormone (ghrelin)

This makes sense to me. We, as a species, haven't had consistent access to food like we do in this modern era. I think we're built to eat less than we currently do, especially in America. Limiting the hours I eat seems to align with how we've lived as humans in the past.

Wrapping up

To wrap it all up, the best diet is the one you can stick to most of the time. If you read between the lines, all three of the top diets are recommending mostly the same menu choices, with some strategic differences. Ultimately, a moderate diet of lower carbs, higher fat, and higher protein is optimal. My recommendation is to pick one, give it hell for a while, then ease into a rhythm that works for you. Once you have experienced tracking your meals and have been mindful of what various choices mean to your caloric and nutrient intake, you'll naturally find yourself making food selections that are far healthier than before. Imagine that, you'll make new habits!

The last thing I'll say is that you should celebrate life! I love food! I mean I love it. All of it. I don't deny myself a greasy, delicious pizza from time to time, nor do I say no to dessert every time it's offered. What's happened over time is that the majority of the time I just decide what I want to eat. I think about which choice I want to make and, for the most part, I choose a healthier option.

Try this next time you're having a meal alone (or if you can talk your partner into this try it together)—eat the meal *consciously*. I learned this at the Kripalu Center for Yoga & Health. Instead of just rushing through the meal, stop and first think about what it took for that food to make it to your plate: the farmer or rancher who grew the items, the delivery folks who brought it to the restaurant (or store), and all the people involved in cooking and serving it to you. It's amazing when you become aware of how much we truly rely on each other to make a meal. Then, after really connecting to that, look at the presentation. Really look at it, and see how the chef intentionally put it on the plate. Slowly take a bite and put the fork down. Let the food just melt in your mouth, slowly chew it, feel the texture of it, the subtle tastes, and then swallow that bite. Pick up the fork and do it again until you've finished the meal. I'm telling you, you'll never be the same once you've mastered this technique. It's not easy! We just rush through meals and never really taste; I mean, really taste what we're eating. Once you master this one, you'll thank me!

8

CANNABIS HISTORY

Even at the dawn of 21st century, 11% of the 252 drugs considered as basic and essential by the WHO were exclusively of flowering plant origin.

Prof. (Dr.) Ciddi Veeresham

My Mom was raised by Christian Scientists. For those of you who aren't familiar with the Christian Science church, they believe in prayer before or instead of medical treatment. For my mom, doctors and medication were the absolute last resort. We used to say she'd wait until a limb was falling off before going to seek treatment. She went most of her life without ever taking any medication. In the end, she developed pancreatic cancer and passed away after a six-month period of failing health. Still she avoided medication. She didn't have any pain medication until the very last hours before her death.

I think my Mom may have been on to something here.

Over the last eighty years, a pervasive undercurrent of distrust has developed over the business of healthcare. This distrust has magnified over the last ten years because of the opioid crisis, which is a direct result of big pharmaceutical companies and their distribution network: the physician community.

The advent of the internet has played a large role in expanding this discontent with western medicine. Access to a world of knowledge has empowered people to ask questions that, in the past, they didn't have the capacity to ask. People want to understand and be an integral part of the healthcare system now.

It doesn't take a rocket scientist to see that the system is skewed in favor of profits over solutions. Drug development research often seeks to alleviate the symptoms but never cure the problem. There are very few examples of drugs that actually cure disease. Most are developed to alleviate the symptoms as long as you continue to take the drug. Antibiotics are an example of a group of drugs that "cure" the disease by killing the bacteria that cause the disease. But in the case of antibiotics, new drugs need to be continually produced to meet the challenge of bacteria which mutate and become resistant to the current antibiotics. In the end, that too is a built in revenue stream, and thank God for that!

To be fair, if I was the CEO of a pharmaceutical company, I would be pushing for profitability as well. It would be my job to increase profits; that's the sole function of a for-profit company. They do a good job at it! The business of pharmaceuticals is lucrative. You have a captive audience of distributors who are taught primarily to push products, and there is a (private and public insurance) system that helps people pay for them. What could be better than that?

Now don't get me wrong, pharmaceutical medicine is an amazing tool in alleviating many issues that people suffer from. My point is that we're becoming more aware of the limitations of pharmaceutical medicine and the not so pretty nature of for-profit healthcare.

People want something different. They want healthcare, not sick care.

Case in point—cannabis medicine.

Let me tell you, I'm the last person you'd think would be an advocate for cannabis. Growing up with that mom who didn't use any drug (legal or illegal) and a father who was a state trooper; you would think I'd be as against cannabis as anyone.

For years I was cannabis agnostic. I couldn't care less. I didn't use it, but I certainly didn't care about someone who did. Having had some experience with it as an adolescent, I knew it was not at all the dangerous drug the government said it was. But because I didn't use it, I really didn't care if it was legalized.

Fast forward to 2016 and the referendum vote on recreational marijuana in Massachusetts. I was active on the board of the American Nurses Association, and we worked with Governor Charlie Baker to oppose the question. I believed some of what was presented by the state government. Enough that I joined in the fight.

So how is it that I am now an outspoken cannabis advocate? Evidence. Logic. Knowledge.

As a nurse we're trained to be skeptical of anything until enough evidence is presented that we can make a logical decision. The problem is that in the US the only evidence is given by a government hell bent on continuing prohibition. Would it surprise you to learn that the government agency responsible for funding cannabis research for the last thirty years has selectively funded only research most likely to provide a negative outcome?

Luckily, I was introduced to the amazing amount of positive research that has been done worldwide. Real, evidence-based, rigorous research. And just like that, my mind was blown.

Welcome to the world of cannabis. Welcome to the beginning of a new world of healthcare. Not a new paradigm, a new world.

Plant-based, holistic, natural medicine, as opposed to refined drug manufacturing, is here and it's not going away. Although a large number of drugs are from plants, the difference is that medicinal drugs are refined down to a single molecule and targeted at specific disease states. The result is, in the case of cannabinoids, the single molecule drugs are far less effective and have many more side effects. Nature has it right, so why change it?

As expected, the entire existing medical complex, from pharma to physicians to government are up in arms over this movement. And with good cause—it's going to disrupt business as usual. It's going to change the world of healthcare. I'm not saying that we shouldn't be cautious and intentional in our use of plant-based medicine. I'm merely saying we should make room for it much quicker than we are. The data is there. The evidence is there. I, for one, am excited for what's possible.

History of Medicinal Cannabis

Cannabis has been used as a medicine, and as a religious tool, for over ten thousand years—we are sure of that. The first recorded use was five thousand years ago by the Chinese. Every major culture since that time has used cannabis as a medicine, because it *is* a medicine. It was an important tool in the arsenal of many doctors in the United States up until 1937. All the major drug companies of the day had cannabis products, and for many years cannabis was listed in the United States Pharmacopeia, the listing of all medicinal drugs used.

So how did it become illegal? Ah, you know how things work in the US, right? Take a guess. Did you guess? It became illegal as a result of blind political ambition and racism. Yes! The all-American way.

Let's set the stage with a little story of America at the beginning of the twentieth century.

In May 1918 in Georgia, a white plantation owner was shot and killed. Known for being abusive, the man had many enemies in the African American community. A black man, Hazel "Hayes" Turner, had an earlier altercation with the plantation owner after the owner had beaten Haye's wife Mary; Hayes was sentenced to a chain gang by an all-white jury. After serving his term, Hayes returned to daily life. Directly after the white man's murder, Hayes was arrested under suspicion of murder. As he was being transported to the county seat, a mob grabbed him and lynched him just outside of town. Later it was determined that Hayes was not involved in the plantation owner's murder—an innocent man had been hung. The following day Mary Turner, Haye's wife, decried her husband's execution and vowed to avenge his death. A crowd kidnapped her, hung her upside down, doused her with gasoline, set her on fire, cut her baby out of her womb, and crushed the baby's head underfoot when he fell to the ground still alive.

This was America in 1918.

To hear the recounting of this reprehensible act stirs anger and indignation today, but that was white America at that time. Not much had changed by the 1930s. What's the connection to marijuana prohibition? You'll see.

Stories abound about motives and actions regarding cannabis prohibition, but here's what we know.

In 1930 Harry J. Anslinger, a veteran of the prohibition of alcohol, was made the first head of the Federal Bureau of Narcotics (FBN). Interestingly this agency was a part of the Department of Treasury. Harry was a smart guy. No flies on him.

Harry was one of the longest serving government officials, heading the FBN until 1962.

The FBN's primary role was to regulate and prosecute infractions related to the Harrison Narcotics Act of 1914, which regulated opium and coca. By the 1930s the population of users had dwindled due to government actions.

In 1933 Harry publicly stated, regarding marijuana, that "There is probably no more absurd fallacy than the idea it makes people violent."

How is it that the man who made this statement in 1933 began a campaign to outlaw marijuana by 1937, using wild stories of murder and mayhem? What motivated such a radical change in his opinion on marijuana? Simple. Job preservation and expansion of his role coupled with outright racism.

Once alcohol prohibition ended, Harry's role was diminished in a big way. The FBN's influence was waning as the opium/coca issue had been brought under control. Harry realized that he had to find something else to focus attention on, something that a large number of people, the right people, were using. Marijuana! That was it. Genius.

From 1933 to 1937, until the Marijuana Tax Act of 1937 was passed, Harry traveled the country lobbying for marijuana prohibition. It couldn't have been a more perfect opportunity for Harry. Here was a whole group of people, hundreds of thousands, who were using a drug Harry had previously thought to be benign. The best part for Harry? They were not white. Bingo! He had his new crusade.

He went from "marijuana is harmless" to saying the following:

> There are 100,000 total marijuana smokers in the US, and most are Negroes, Hispanics, Filipinos and entertainers. Their Satanic music, jazz and swing, result from marijuana usage. This marijuana causes white women to seek sexual relations with Negroes, entertainers and any others.

> The primary reason to outlaw marijuana is its effect on the degenerate races.

> I wish I could show you what a small marihuana cigarette can do to one of our degenerate Spanish-speaking residents. That's why our problem is so great; the greatest percentage of our population is composed of Spanish-speaking persons, most of who are low mentally, because of social and racial conditions.

> Marihuana leads to pacifism and communist brainwashing.

Reefer makes darkies think they're as good as white men (McDonald 2017).

As you can clearly see, these statements were meant to strike fear into the white population. Harry created a file of cases from around the country that he used to cite as examples of what cannabis could do when consumed. The problem was that none of it was true. He changed facts and stories to suit his agenda.

It's well known that Harry enlisted the help of media mogul William Randolph Hearst in his efforts. Stories abound about Hearst's motivation: the threat of hemp to his timber interests or his dislike of the Mexican community. In the end, it was most likely motivated by simple greed. Hearst owned most of the newspaper outlets of the day, and what sells papers? Fear! Controversy!

By 1937 Harry had convinced most of the nation and congress that marijuana had to be outlawed. Was any of it based on science? Any of it based on truth? No. Not one bit.

As a matter of fact, who do you think was vehemently opposed to this action? None other than the American Medical Association (AMA)! That's right—the physicians opposed this. The head of legal counsel for the AMA testified before Congress prior to the passing of the Marijuana Tax Act and voiced their opposition, saying it was a grave mistake to limit the use and research potential of such a beneficial medicine. Think about it: these physicians had been using cannabis as a medicine their entire careers—with great success!

Despite this opposition, Congress was convinced to pass the Marijuana Tax Act, and just like that an entire segment of our citizenry became the focus of eighty years of persecution.

Do you think the racism was limited to just the 1930's? Fast forward to 1970 and to none other than Richard Milhous Nixon, former President of the United States. He built his whole platform on the War on Drugs.

Nixon's administration was responsible for the scheduling of drugs, including cannabis, under the Controlled Substances Act (CSA). Here's a little-known fact: the reason they did this was in response to Timothy Leary successfully defending himself against a marijuana possession charge. The Supreme Court declared the Marijuana Tax Act unconstitutional as a result of Mr. Leary's defense.

In response, the Feds created the CSA and marijuana became a Schedule I drug. Under the Drug Enforcement Administration scheduling system, a Schedule 1 drug has the following characteristics:

A. The drug or other substance has a high potential for abuse.
B. The drug or other substance has no currently accepted medical use in treatment in the United States.
C. There is a lack of accepted safety for use of the drug or other substance under medical supervision.

I hope you're starting to see the hypocrisy of our government here. Cannabis, as proven by firm scientific evidence, does not meet ANY of those criteria. As an aside, pouring more fuel on the fire, guess who owns the only patent in the United States for cannabis as a medicine, filed in 2003? Oh, you know the answer already . . . you can sense the hypocrisy of it . . . yes, the United States Government.

What was Nixon's motivation? Again, racism at its finest. He hated black people and the anti-war movement, two groups who were users of marijuana. Nixon was adamant with all his drug folks—under no circumstances would marijuana ever be legalized. It gets worse: Nixon convened a commission to research marijuana and present recommendations. The commission's recommendation? Legalize marijuana, but Nixon ignored it, of course.

In an interview published years later, John Ehrlichman, Nixon's domestic policy chief, went on the record about the administrations real motivation behind drug criminalization:

> "The Nixon campaign in 1968, and the Nixon White House after that, had two enemies: the antiwar left and black people," former Nixon domestic policy chief John Ehrlichman told Harper's writer Dan Baum for the April cover story published Tuesday.

> "You understand what I'm saying? We knew we couldn't make it illegal to be either against the war or black, but by getting the public to associate the hippies with marijuana and blacks with heroin. And then criminalizing both heavily, we could disrupt those communities," Ehrlichman said. "We could arrest their leaders. raid their homes, break up their meetings, and vilify them night after night on the evening news. Did we know we were lying about the drugs? Of course we did" (LoBianco 2016).

Understanding the history of racism and political ambition coupled with the science of medicinal cannabis has motivated me in my quest to educate everyone else and to push for an end to this ridiculous prohibition.

Today

Where are we today? Thirty-three states have passed laws broadly legalizing medical cannabis. In addition, eleven states and the District of Columbia have authorized recreational use of cannabis.

And still our government at the federal level continues to persecute our fellow Americans. Any guesses as to why? Well, you have twelve thousand DEA agents who don't ever want to see any drug legalized for the same reason Harry Anslinger started the whole campaign—job preservation.

Let's not forget the folks who have spent over thirty billion dollars lobbying our politicians—the pharmaceutical companies. Do you think they want to see cannabis allowed to take the place of a good piece of their revenue stream? Oh, hell no! The generation of physicians who used cannabis as an effective medicine are long dead and gone. The physicians of today have been trained in rigid pharmaceutical treatment strategies. It's going to take time to move the needle toward full acceptance in the medical community.

It's time to recognize that the War on Drugs is an abject failure. We spend over fifty billion dollars a year on this fanciful war with little results to show for it. Instead of persecuting our brothers and sisters, perhaps we should spend that money creating economic opportunity and getting rid of the reasons people resort to selling and using drugs in the first place. When you have no hope, you do hopeless things. It's time, my friends, it's time to right the wrongs. It's time for all of us to stand up, like those brave, young souls did in the late '60s and put an end to this unwinnable war.

9

Cannabis: The (Not So) New Medicine

The evidence is overwhelming that marijuana can
relieve certain types of pain, nausea, vomiting, and other
symptoms caused by such illnesses as multiple sclerosis,
cancer and AIDS—or by the harsh drugs sometimes used
to treat them. And it can do so with remarkable safety.
Indeed, marijuana is less toxic than many of the drugs
that physicians prescribe every day.

Dr. Joycelyn Elders, Former US Surgeon General

As I mentioned in an earlier chapter, I am the last guy you'd expect
to be advocating for cannabis. Yet here I am at the forefront of the
burgeoning cannabis industry. Why the complete change of heart?
Evidence. I have taken a two-year deep dive into the world of cannabis
research and training, and there is a lot of it, and have become
convinced of the powerful abilities of this plant to alleviate many of
our ills. This is legitimate, so much so that I'm currently enrolled in the
first Master of Science in Cannabis Science and Therapeutics program
in the world at the University of Maryland School of Pharmacy.

Those of us in healthcare are trained to evaluate things with a bit of skepticism. We operate in an environment of evidence-based practice. It makes sense. We don't want to run off trying new things without understanding if it will have a positive or negative effect. You can see why, in the beginning of my cannabis experience, I was highly skeptical of the claims being made. Initially, I disbelieved the sheer amount of potential areas cannabis could positively affect human health and well-being How could one plant be so effective in treating so many different symptoms?

Once I really understood the underlying biology behind cannabis use and effects, it all made perfect sense. Let's dive into the explanations of cannabis potency.

Endocannabinoid System (ECS)

I'll try to keep this biochemistry light for my non-chemistry friends, but I do so love to dive deep!

In the late 1980s researchers discovered that there were specific cannabinoid receptors in mammals. This naturally led to the search for endogenous (created within the organism) cannabinoids that bound to these receptors. It didn't take long before researchers discovered the first of many endocannabinoids.

The two primary endocannabinoids, Anandamide and 2-AG have been subjects of research experiments since that time. Because of their lipophilic (oil-loving) nature, they are created in the body when needed and then quickly degraded and excreted, unlike other neurotransmitters, such as serotonin and dopamine, which are hydrophilic (water loving) and are produced and stored in the body for use when needed.

The endocannabinoids are chemically similar to the phytocannabinoids (plant-derived cannabinoids) found in cannabis, hence the ability of cannabis to elicit an effect when introduced into the body.

The cannabis plant contains over 150 different identified cannabinoids and over 1,400 chemical compounds in total. There are over 550 different strains of cannabis with varying chemical makeups.

The two primary phytocannabinoids are THC, which is the cannabinoid that produces the "high," and CBD, the nonintoxicating cannabinoid.

The discovery of the ECS will be heralded as one of the greatest medical discoveries of the twentieth century. It's directly involved in the maintenance of homeostasis. Homeostasis is the dynamic state of equilibrium maintaining optimum bodily function.

Homeostasis is the equilibrium maintained by all systems within an organism. Your body uses many different mechanisms and systems to maintain that balance. For example, your body temperature needs to be kept relatively close to 98.6°F, the pH level of your blood must be kept within a very narrow range (7.35-7.45) to survive and function, and blood pressure must be maintained in a tight range to support life.

Relaxing	The ECS works with the other neurotransmitter systems (dopamine, serotonin, gaba) to decrease depression and anxiety (Mahenthiran 2019).
Eating	The ECS helps to regulate and increase our appetite. One of the first approved uses of cannabinoid therapy was for AIDS and cancer patients to stimulate their appetites (Jager and Witkamp 2014).

Sleeping   The ECS plays a large role in sleep regulation. It's effects can be seen in promoting both wakefulness and sleep (Murillo-Rodríguez 2008).

Forgetting   The ECS plays a role in modulating the memory. A prime example is the ability of the ECS to affect the retention and recall of stressful events. Recent studies have shown that cannabinoids can alleviate the harsh symptoms of PTSD, which include continually reliving the memory of the traumatic event. The ECS acts as an emotional buffer in stressful moments (Morena and Compolongo 2014).

Protecting   A multitude of research studies have shown the ECS to be instrumental in protecting homeostasis in the body. From promoting the auto-programmed death of rogue cells to providing protection to various cells in the body (Acharya et al. 2017).

Imagine all that built into one massive system? Your ECS is the largest neurotransmitter receptor system in your body. If you added up all the other neuroreceptors in your body, they still wouldn't equal the amount of ECS receptors.

There are multiple cannabinoid receptors. The CB1 and CB2 receptors were identified first and have been studied the most.

CB1 receptors are found throughout your body but primarily reside in the brain. THC, the intoxicating component of cannabis, binds to the CB1 receptor. It makes sense that most of the CB1 receptors reside in the brain, hence the "high" from THC.

Can you die from an overdose of cannabis? No. That's a hard no. The reason is simple, and it's best explained by giving you the opioid example. Currently in this country approximately fifty thousand people a year die from opiate overdose. How does it happen? What's the cause of death? They stop breathing. Opiates effect the respiratory center in the brainstem due to the presence of opioid receptors. They very literally stop breathing. As a matter of fact, as nurses we're trained when giving any opiate to watch the patient for the first half hour to hour for any change in respiration. Cannabis, and THC particularly, has little to no effect on respiration. The reason really is simple—there are no CB1 receptors in the brain stem for THC to bind to, so basic functions like respiration rate remain unaffected.

CB2 receptors are primarily distributed throughout the immune system and peripheral nervous system. These receptors are active in immune response, inflammatory response, and other systemic homeostatic processes.

The role of the ECS and cannabinoids is to mediate the release of other neurotransmitters and chemicals in the body. That's one of the reasons they are effective across a wide spectrum of things within the human body.

The distribution and the interaction of these receptors is widespread. Are you starting to see the many ways cannabis can be therapeutic in the body?

The Plant

For over ten thousand years, cannabis has been used by people around the world as a medicine. Until 1937 it was used by physicians in this the Unites States, and it was outlawed for nonmedical, nonscientific reasons.

There are three primary types of cannabis plants: *Cannabis sativa*, *Cannabis indica*, and *Cannabis ruderalis*. *C. sativa* and *C. indica* are cultivated commercially today for their medicinal and recreational value. *C. ruderalis* grows wild and has not been commercially cultivated.

Hemp is a *C. sativa* derivative that produces a plant with a much lower THC content than standard *C. sativa*. As a matter of fact, for hemp to be legal in the United States, it has to contain less than .3 percent THC. Anything over .3 percent and that crop has to be destroyed.

Hemp has been cultivated for centuries around the world. The first bible, printed by Guttenberg, was on hemp paper. Betsy Ross used hemp cloth for the first US flag. If you came to the new world back in the early days before the revolutionary war, you were required to grow hemp. This versatile, sustainable plant has an amazing list of uses.

Again, cannabis contains over one hundred or more cannabinoids and possibly up to fourteen hundred total chemical compounds. Some have been identified while others have yet to be elucidated.

All varieties of cannabis contain varying levels of THC. Cannabidiol (CBD) has received the lion's share of interest to date for two main reasons: (1) studies have shown CBD to be effective in treating a multitude of issues we experience and (2) its nonintoxicating nature is more palatable to a wider audience.

Along with the cannabinoids, as mentioned above, there is a plethora of chemical compounds. For example, currently there is a great deal of interest in the resident terpenes in the cannabis plant. Terpenes are found in many plants. They are created as a means of defense. Terpenes are responsible for the smells associated with the plants, and so the distinct aroma of the cannabis plant is due to its terpenes. (Fun fact: beta-caryophyllene [a terpene] is common to both the cannabis plant and black pepper. Drug sniffing dogs are trained using black pepper; so maybe don't carry a lot of black pepper when walking through the airport.)

Using Cannabis

If you've been around cannabis at all these days, you've heard about the difference between the effects of *sativa* and *indica*. *Sativa* is known to be uplifting and *indica* has a reputation for producing more of a bodily sensation. The difference in effect is related to the varying amount of chemicals resident in each. THC is THC. The unique mix of cannabinoids, terpenes, flavonoids, and other chemicals produces different results for different people. Again, remember that there are over five hundred fifty different varieties of cannabis plants with different chemical makeups.

You may have also heard about something called the entourage effect. It's a real thing folks. The *entourage effect* is about the interaction between the chemical components of each cannabis strain within the human body, and it's real. We're early on in where this plant is going. What we know for certain already is that it's safer than most other medications and effective in a wide-variety of instances. The entourage effect is as follows: it's the interaction of all the resident chemical components of the particular cannabis plant that increase the effect of each of the other components.

Let's take the CBD industry for example. CBD is the nonintoxicating cannabinoid in cannabis. A dizzying array of products have been marketed as of late, and many of them use the term "full spectrum." Full spectrum, broad spectrum, isolate—these are important terms to know. Full spectrum is just that. During the extraction process—and not all extraction processes are equal—all of the available cannabinoids and ancillary chemical components are extracted and appear in the end product, which is usually an oil. This includes the legal .3 percent of THC as well as all other resident components. Broad spectrum products have simply had the THC removed during the extraction process. Isolates are just as the name implies: only CBD is extracted, and all other components are stripped off.

Why does this matter? It goes back to the entourage effect. The effects of the various components are enhanced and increased if taken all together. Do we know why? Nope. Does it matter at this point? Not in my book (literally). There have been studies that have shown that, over time, taking CBD isolate, without the other components, leads to decreasing effectiveness of the CBD. A recent article in Frontiers of Neurology spoke about this phenomenon in people being treated with both CBD isolate and CBD-rich Cannabis Extracts for treatment-resistant seizures (Pamplona, Rolim da Silva, and Coan 2018). Your body builds up a tolerance to straight CBD isolate. Tolerance is a rather common occurrence with pharmaceuticals. Makes sense since pharmaceutical are made by isolating distinct drug molecules. No entourage effect there. Including all components in the end product increases the drug's medicinal potency and potential duration of effect as well.

Why use cannabis? Because it's safe, effective, and natural. So, how do people use it?

Smoking

There are several ways to get cannabinoids into your body. First, and the one we all know about, is smoking. Being a nurse, I'm not a fan of smoking anything. Having been addicted to cigarettes for many years, I know the harmful effects of smoking tobacco. I've also cared for many patients suffering with chronic obstructive pulmonary disease (COPD), the overarching medical term for a lot of lung disease states. It's awful having COPD. Ask someone who has it. Tobacco use is the number one cause of COPD. However, and this is big, smoking cannabis appears to have no link to COPD. A recent study showed no causal link between smoking cannabis and COPD (Ribeiro, and Ind 2016). Is it the beneficial effects of the cannabinoids? That remains to be seen, but what we know is smoking cannabis is completely different than smoking tobacco. Smoking or vaping cannabis is a great route of administration for anyone who needs immediate relief. When you smoke cannabis, the THC, and other cannabinoids, are deposited directly into the bloodstream, bypassing the *first-pass effect* (which I'll talk about in a moment). Smoking results in up to 30 percent bioavailability, which is how much of the cannabinoids are available to be used by the body after ingestion.

Sublingual

Taking oils sublingually, under the tongue, results in a bit of absorption directly into the bloodstream, but most of the product follows the route of digestion/metabolization when swallowed. You see a lot of CBD oils on the market today, and this is how they're used.

Edibles

Edibles deliver the product through the digestive system. Almost everything we swallow is metabolized by our liver. Metabolization is a really cool process that the body uses to break down substances it recognizes as not normally part of the system. Drugs fall into this category of "things not part of the body" and the metabolization process breaks them down, converts them chemically, and makes them more hydrophilic and easier for the kidneys to dispose of. During the metabolization process, delta-9 THC, which is resident in cannabis and produces the "high," is converted to another chemical—11-hydroxy THC. 11-Hydroxy is far more potent and longer lasting than delta-9 THC. When you smoke cannabis, delta-9 THC is delivered directly into the bloodstream and produces the effect. It only lasts a couple hours at best because it's delta-9 THC and that's what it does chemically in the body. 11-Hydroxy THC lasts 6–8 hours and can produce a much more intoxicating effect. One important difference between smoking and eating cannabis is the bioavailability of cannabinoids. Bioavailability is decreased 4–12 percent due to the metabolization process during digestion.

Topicals

Topicals are commonly in use for localized pain relief or skin care. Studies have shown that the cannabinoids (THC/CBD) don't reach the bloodstream and only have a very localized effect when applied topically. Considering your skin is your largest organ, and the first line of defense, healthy skin is kind of important. The fact that your skin has a large amount of cannabinoid receptors makes using cannabis products topically a good idea.

Why are people using cannabis?

I'm fifty-seven glorious years old now. I know, thank you, I don't look like it at all. Good genes and lots of work. But, shit still hurts.

I've started to make an involuntary noise now when exiting a vehicle. Like a grunt of sorts. What the hell is that all about? Is it an effort to get out of the car now? Ha! I used to discount what my elders said when they were complaining about the aches and pains of aging. Certainly that was never going to happen to me! Well, it has happened. You may have figured out by now that I stay super active, always on the move, working out regularly. All that takes its toll. Like I said, stuff hurts. Not only does that affect me during the day, but it also affects my sleep. It's true. When I roll over, the aches and pains wake me up.

Cannabis to the rescue!

I use both CBD and THC in combination. Remember earlier in the book, in the chapter on nutrition, I mentioned how important tracking your food intake is? I also track my sleep using an app. I've done it for several years now. I started prior to using cannabis, and I have hard data that shows what a profoundly positive effect cannabis has on my sleep. This is no little thing. Sleep is critical to good health. A lack of good sleep can cause all sorts of long-term health issues.

Another very common use of cannabis, both for recreation and medical cannabis, is to relieve anxiety. Sure, it relieves everyday stress, but I'm talking about mental distress, the kind of anxiety that effects your everyday life. I've experienced periods of extreme anxiety over the course of my life. I've had panic attacks (if you have never had one count yourself lucky). They say panic attacks are similar to the feeling experienced when having a heart attack. The worst part is, you never know when it's going to happen. Oh, you can feel when it's coming on, but the timing of when that starts is a mystery. It's a strange feeling as it starts to wind up. Awful, just awful. Cannabis, both CBD and THC, have been shown to alleviate anxiety with little to no side effects.

One note—cannabinoids are known to be biphasic, which means that a low dose can do one thing (calm, soothe, exhilarate) and a higher dose can cause a diametrically different effect (paranoia, panic, anxiety). I hear stories all the time from folks who haven't used cannabis in years who try it, mostly using edibles, and have a panic attack. It's because of a too high—no pun intended—dose of THC. The cannabis plants today have been bred with five times the THC content of past plants.

For that reason, I'm a huge proponent of the microdosing of any cannabinoid, whether THC or CBD. Whatever your preference is, using the smallest amount to achieve the desired effect is most beneficial.

Pain relief is another very common use for cannabis. Both THC and CBD have pain relieving qualities. If you're in a state where you have access to both, a combination, most likely in oil format, is preferred. Think of the entourage effect again here. Taking both THC and CBD together in a microdose form allows for the beneficial effects to work in combination. If you're worried about the intoxicating effects of THC, it's good to note that CBD has shown to have a mediating effect on the intoxicating aspects of THC. If you're in a state where recreational use is illegal, and you don't qualify for a medical card full spectrum CBD is the way to go. This isn't going to be like taking a Percocet, or some other opiate, where you'll feel the effect strongly. Cannabis will have a much better effect over the long-term without the awful side effects of opiates, but you won't have that sensation you have with opiates, which in my book is a good thing. Less of a dopamine trigger, less addictive. Bingo!

What's my favorite route of administration? Edibles for sure. They last longer, and I don't have that intoxicating feeling (unless I choose to) with microdosing. For me, smoking or vaping introduces too much delta-9 THC at once, and it's not fun for me.

Legally Accessing Cannabis

There are over thirty states with a medical cannabis program. Thirty-plus states have recognized the medicinal value of cannabis, and still our federal government clings to prohibition. By the people, for the people? Yeah, I think not! Add another eleven states, plus the District of Columbia (yes, that's right, cannabis is legal in our nation's capital), to the list as having medical and recreational programs.

Medical marijuana programs, still using that old stigmatic word instead of the scientific label of cannabis, have very defined criteria used to determine if someone is eligible for the program. Each state has differing criteria, which is a bit nutty, no? Welcome to the world of cannabis medicine. For instance, in Massachusetts you have to certify as having one of the following conditions (Massachusetts Department of Public Health 2020):

Qualified conditions in Massachusetts include:

- Cancer
- Glaucoma
- Acquired immune deficiency syndrome (AIDS) or HIV positive status

- Hepatitis C
- Amyotrophic lateral sclerosis (ALS)
- Crohn's disease
- Parkinson's disease
- Multiple sclerosis

There are other debilitating conditions, as determined in writing by a qualified physician, which may include:

- Chronic back pain
- Rheumatoid Arthritis
- Insomnia
- Anorexia
- Anxiety
- Depression

As mentioned, the list of conditions varies by state.

It's a wonderful step in the right direction, but there are issues with the whole system.

First, you have to find a doctor willing to certify you. It's becoming easier, but it's not cheap. Also, people are unwilling to even begin the discussion with their primary providers and be entered into any system that documents anything related to cannabis in their health record. And with good reason. Have you ever known a government agency or health insurance company to use any information for your benefit? Oh, hell no!

Speaking of health insurance—none of this is covered. It's all out of pocket here. Will that ever change? Your guess is as good as mine.

Logically, the insurance companies could save millions of dollars a year by covering cannabis care, but bureaucracies move ever so slowly.

If you're in a state where recreational is legal, you're a little better off, but still there are issues. It goes back to the hypocrisy of our government's view of cannabis. Here's a perfect example of what I'm talking about: I can walk into a thousand different places and purchase alcohol for personal consumption. Alcohol is a known carcinogen and poisonous to the human body. Over eighty thousand people a year die from this drug, yet I can go in, show my ID to confirm my age, and walk out with a bottle of poison that has no childproof top on it. What's the experience when I go to a dispensary in a recreational state? I show my ID a minimum of two, sometimes three times; each time it's documented on computer and enters a database somewhere. How will that information be used? Why does my purchase need to be tracked so closely?

I have to question why one drug, of known harm, is so freely available, and another with documented positive benefits, requires that my purchase be documented in a state database.

What about our elderly population? They're the least likely to have a conversation with their doctor about cannabis, but the elderly population is the demographic who would benefit the most! It's virtually impossible for these folks to gain access to cannabis, for a myriad of reasons. And yet, the average elderly person takes over five pharmaceutical drugs a day, and it jumps to over seven for someone in a nursing home (*MD Magazine 2010*). The biggest hurdle now is facilities who accept federal reimbursement, which is all of them, typically do not allow any cannabis on premise.

I could go on and on about what we know about cannabis, both THC and CBD, but there are many very informative books on the subject. I've included a list of great reads in the appendix at the end of this book.

10

Bringing it All Together

Transformation literally means going beyond your form.

Wayne Dyer

It's work being absolutely fucking amazing. Don't let me fool you. It takes work to grasp the reasons why you can't be who you really are—the most magnificent person you'll ever know! I hope you got a sense of that after reading through the preceding chapters.

We talked about the mental and physical aspects of living the most amazing life. All these are required aspects for creating that life. But what's the end result? What's the secret at the end of the rainbow? What are the fruits of your labor?

Love. Love of life, love of others, and most importantly, love of self.

Now you may believe that you have all these in good measure, but experience tells me that the love you're most likely lacking is self-love.

Perhaps even the words *self-love* conjures an image of a selfish, narcissistic person only concerned with their own desires and wishes—that's part of your own negative self-view popping up.

Remember, we're wired with an inherent negative bias. We tend to view things from a negative perspective. This includes us! Not only are *you* the one *you* talk to the most, but I guarantee your self-talk is mostly from a negative perspective. It's how we're wired. There is no escaping it. But . . . you can accept it and learn to love it. To love yourself . . .

What's available when you truly, absolutely love yourself? It's almost indescribable. Once you get who you really are and love yourself completely, only then can you turn that outward and love everything else around you, including those you profess to love already. I mean you'll really, truly be available to love them exactly as they are.

After my last relationship ended over a year ago, I went through a very traumatic, emotional period of deep introspection. I mean I turned over all sorts of rocks trying to figure out why a relationship that I had invested so much time, money, and energy in had failed, yet again.

I worked with some fabulous therapists around such things as attachment theory, which is determined in the first eighteen months of life and dictates how you attach to others in a relationship. All good there, to my surprise. Then we looked at schema therapy and personality theory. Combining the new insights with *all* the things I've learned over the last thirty years about self-improvement, I came to the conclusion that love, for me, was very much a conditional experience.

For those of you who know me personally, you know since my divorce ten years ago I have dated a lot of amazing, beautiful women. A few I was actually engaged to for a brief time. Every one of them was perfect exactly as they were.

So why haven't I had a long-term relationship? Although I said to myself and everyone around me that I intended to embody love in every situation, the love had conditions attached. It all came down to one simple fact—I did not love me. Instead of validating myself, I relied on the other person to validate me. When I received positive feedback, I was in heaven; when there was anything that looked like criticism, that five-year-old emotional child reacted like a five-year-old. Fascinating stuff, right?? Fuck yes, it is!

Using the various tools we've talked about, I've become aware of who I *really* am and completely love who I am.

What's been the result of that awareness? For the first time, since I began dating at the age of fifteen, I've been able to be with just me for the last year. Truly, for the first time in my entire dating life, I haven't had to have to be with someone to validate who I am in the world. That is the freedom of being absolutely fucking amazing!

How will the next relationship be? Totally and completely unlike any other I've had, that's for sure. I no longer need external validation; the pressure is off the other person to provide it. I can simply enjoy my partner for who they are and not what my partner can provide me. Wow, I'm excited about the possibilities!

Ok, got it now? Becoming absolutely fucking amazing (AFA) is the best thing you can ever do.

Here are the seven practices that will lead to an AFA life!

1. Meditation—15 mins each morning
2. Sun Salutations—a short series of morning yoga poses
3. 10/10/10—thirty minutes of mental exercises for positive thinking and positive being

4. Exercise—a minimum of three times a week
5. Nutrition—log your meals and maintain consistency
6. Cannabis—as needed, as desired, micro dosing THC/CBD
7. Being—live outside meaning

That's it; that's' all you have to do. Easy right? Yes!

Meditation

Anyone can do it. It's the basis for creating the life you love and the life that loves you. Meditate and you will be AFA.

Understand that everyone has an unceasing stream of thoughts. Everyone. It's the human condition. It's normal.

Begin by finding a spot where you can sit uninterrupted for a few minutes before your day begins. Start with a five-minute moment of just sitting still. Seriously, just sit there and notice what's going on. Notice your thoughts, the noises in the house, what's going on with your body: tightness. pain, etc. Do this for a week. Be patient—if you walk straight into the woods for thirty years and turn around to walk out, it's not going to be a quick walk back. Take your time. Gradually, each week, add another five minutes to your sitting. Once you get to fifteen minutes, you can start to focus on your thoughts a bit more. You can start to notice when your thoughts stray, and you can bring them back to a focal point; most people use the breath as a focal point since it's rhythmic and automatic.

You'll find more resources about meditation at the end of the book.

Sun Salutations

This simple yogic series is the perfect way to wake up your body and get ready for your day. You can do this before meditating, if you'd like, or afterward. It should be one of the first two things you do each day. If you'd like, you can add in the following simple routine designed to offset our sedentary lifestyle. Add or delete any movements. I'm a huge fan of dynamic movement (it goes back to my Ashtanga yoga teaching days). Moving in and out of specific yoga postures slowly and with intention, works really well to warm up your body after lying in bed all night.

Here's what I do:

- Modified Sun Salutation—seven times.
- Cat-Cow Alternating—seven times.
- Child-Cobra Alternating—seven times.
- Pigeon Pose—hold for seven breaths each side.
- Bridge Pose-Knee to Chest Alternating—seven times.
- Revolved Abdomen Pose—lying on your back, bend legs 90 degrees, and allow them to drop to one side. Stretch your arms out in a T formation to increase the stretch if desired. To complete the "wringing out" of your entire spine, you can turn your head and face the opposite direction from where your knees are pointing. Hold for seven breaths. Slowly unwind in the opposite order: first slowly turn your head back to center. Reach your opposite hand over to the top knee and help your knees back up to center 90 degrees. Now do the same in the opposite direction.
- Savasana-Corpse pose—lying on your back, let your arms lengthen out beside you and relax everything. Let your body

sink into the floor and let your mouth drop open. Stay here for a as long as you'd like, letting thoughts just flow without stopping to consider them. Just relax.

10/10/10

My friend Warren Rustand, an amazing human being and mentor to many of the world's top entrepreneurs, shared this at a leadership conference I attended in Washington, D.C., earlier this year. I've used a similar format for over ten years, and I find it foundational to creating the life I lead.

Here's the magic 10/10/10 formula:

- For one minute, ask yourself "Why am I alive today?"
- For ten minutes, have grateful and positive thoughts. I like to use affirmations; one that I use every day is from *The Big Leap* by Gay Hendricks. Every day I say, "I expand in success, abundance, and love as I inspire those around me to do the same". This says it all for me.
- For ten minutes, read inspirational Books—whatever you find inspiring.
- For ten minutes, write positive thoughts in your journal. Gratitude is a good place to start. Write down a few things you're grateful for. There is always something!

Exercise

In addition to using yoga every morning as a warm up for your day, regular exercise will change your life. If you want to live longer, if you want to enjoy your life to the fullest, you have to exercise. You know my preference—HIIT, high-intensity interval training. Just choose what works for you and get busy. The current data shows that a minimum of three hours per week of movement and exercise produces lasting results. I recommend using a heart rate monitor and app to track your heart rate variability (HRV). HRV is the time in between heart beats and is a great way to monitor the positive effects of exercise (and all that you do toward creating a healthy lifestyle). An article in the Harvard Medical School publication describes why HRV is an important measure of health (Campos 2017). Whatever the form of exercise, it's your choice. Just get busy!

Nutrition

Exercise is important, but nutrition is far more important. What you eat affects every aspect of your body. What you eat quite literally dictates your well-being. In "Chapter 6: You are What You Eat" I've given you an overview of various diets; however, most diets follow the same principles. So, my number one dieting advice is to you is *track your meals!*

Cannabis

Safe, effective, natural. This plant supports a healthy lifestyle. You'll start to see increasing negative talk in the very near future — understand that this talk is fabricated by those who stand to lose revenue. Plain and simple. The time is here for you and me to take control and responsibility for our healthcare, and cannabis can go a long way to keep us healthy and happy.

BEING

This is the big one! Living outside of meaning is just that. Life is lived outside of your head, but we live as if our concept of reality, which is generated in our head, is *the* reality. Life happens, occurs, outside of you, and life has no inherent meaning. In other words, you can, and do, make up the meaning of every single experience you have, and your experience of life is all based on your past. Your whole life is lived in comparison to past events and experiences. By living outside meaning, you encounter life moment by moment "as-lived"— "as-experienced." Life approached from this perspective makes anything possible, in any situation (I first encountered this transformative concept from Landmark Worldwide).

This last practice—*being*— is the real deal. All the self-help, therapy, yoga, and meditation has gone into cultivating the ability to let go of having to make meaning out of everything. Believe me, I make meaning every single moment of every single day—it's what we do as humans. We can't escape that inevitability. But I have cultivated the ability to be aware of the meaning I make and choose an alternate meaning, or at least consider alternate meanings, in the moment. You can do it too! That's the power of just simply being.

That is all there is to it. Simple, effective, and achievable. All you need to do now is simply decide to begin. Every journey starts with the first step. This is not a quick fix program. It's not a sprint: it's a marathon. Each day you move a little closer to creating that magnificent life you dream of. Each day of practice will lead you to that moment when you can say, without any reservation, "I AM ABSOLUTELY FUCKING AMAZING!"

Appendix

Meditation

I've used a lot of different apps that provide all sorts of guided meditations and tips and tricks. My favorite of all is from a remarkable human being and personal friend, Dandapani. His commitment to bringing love and peace to the world through his sharing of age-old wisdom is built into everything he does. Check out his website and try the free app (www.dandapani.org).

Another app I've used and liked is Insight Timer. There's lots of content to choose from, and the app works flawlessly.

Nutrition Tracking

There are many apps available to track your daily nutrition. Some are specific to the particular nutrition plan you're using. Here are three of my favorites:

- www.loseit.com
- www.myfitnesspal.com
- apps.apple.com/us/app/carb-manager-keto-diet-app/id410089731

Movement

The websites below offer general information, videos, classes, and content related to each specific genre:

- www.crossfit. com
- www.kripalu.org
- www.easytaichi.com
- www.vagabondcrossfit.com

Cannabis

- Watch the TED talk on YouTube: A Doctor's Case for Medical Marijuana by David Casarett (https://www.youtube. com/watch?v=0ygtX2nyexo)
- *Marijuana: A Short History* by Hudak, John
- *Pain-Free with CBD: Everything You Need to Know to Safely and Effectively Use Cannabidiol* by Alice O'Leary Randall and Eloise Theise
- *Healing with CBD: How Cannabidiol Can Transform Your Health without the High:* by Eileen Konieczny RN with Lauren Wilson

Transformational Education

- Landmark Worldwide (www.landmarkworldwide.com)
- Kripalu Center for Yoga & Health (www.kripalu.org)

References

Acharya, Nandini, Sasi Penukonda, Tatiana Shcheglova, Adam T. Hagymasi, Sreyashi Basu, and Pramod K. Srivastava. 2017. "Endocannabinoid System Acts as A Regulator of Immune Homeostasis in The Gut." 114 (19). https://doi.org/ 10.1073/pnas.1612177114

Anslinger, Harry J. 1933. "Organized Protection Against Organized Predatory Crime: VI. Peddling of Narcotic Drugs". *Journal of Criminal Law and Criminology* (1931-1951) 24 (3): 636. https://doi:10.2307/1135776.

Campos, Marcelo. 2017. "Heart Rate Variability: A New Way to Track Well-Being." *Harvard Health Blog*. https://www. health.harvard.edu/blog/heart-rate-variability-new-way-track-well-2017112212789.

Centers for Disease Control and Prevention. n.d. "Adult Obesity Causes & Consequences." Overweight & Obesity. https://www.cdc.gov/obesity/ adult/ \causes.html.

Coila, Bridget. 2018. "Monounsaturated Fat Vs. Polyunsaturated Fat." Livestrong.com. https://www. livestrong.com/article/85085-monounsaturated-fat-vs.-polyunsaturated-fat.

CrossFit. 2019. "Major Victory for CrossFit: Judge Orders Terminating and Massive Monetary Sanctions Against The NSCA." *CrossFit.com, December 4, 2019.* https:// www.CrossFit.com/battles/major-victory-for-CrossFit-judge-orders-terminating-and-massive-monetary-sanctions-against-the-nsca.

Department of Public Health. 2020. "Guidance for Physicians regarding the Medical Use of Marijuana." *The Commonwealth of Massachusetts.* https://www.mass.gov/files/documents/2016/07/rw/physician-guidance-2015-06-09.pdf?_ga=2.185618027.310654155.1581632701-2138704902.1577471859.

Drug Enforcement Administration. 2020. "Drug Scheduling." https://www.dea.gov /drug-scheduling.

Gotink, Rinske A., Meike W. Vernooij, M. Arfan Ikram, Wiro J. Niessen, Gabriel P. Krestin, Albert Hofman, Henning Tiemeier, and M. G. Myriam Hunink. 2018. "Meditation and Yoga Practice Are Associated with Smaller Right Amygdala Volume: The Rotterdam Study". *Brain Imaging and Behavior* 12 (6): 1631-1639. https://doi.org/10.1007/s11682-018-9826-z.

Hyde, Bruce, and Drew Kopp. 2019. *Speaking Being: Werner Erhard, Martin Heidegger, and a New Possibility of Being Human.* New Jersey: John Wiley & Sons.

Jager, Gerry, and Renger F. Witkamp. 2014. "The Endocannabinoid System and Appetite: Relevance for Food Reward". *Nutrition Research Reviews* 27 (1): 172-185. https://doi:10.1017/s0954422414000080.

Jiménez-Maldonado, Alberto, Iván Rentería, Patricia C. García-Suárez, José Moncada-Jiménez, and Luiz Fernando Freire-Royes. "The Impact of High-Intensity Interval Training on Brain Derived Neurotrophic Factor in Brain: A Mini-Review", 2020. https://www.ncbi.nlm. nih.gov/pmc/articles/PMC6246624/.

Kabat-Zinn, Jon. 2004. *Wherever You Go, There You Are.* London: Piatkus

Libet, Benjamin, Curtis A. Gleason, Elwood W. Wright, and Dennis K. Pearl. 1983. "Time of Conscious Intention to Act in Relation to Onset of Cerebral Activity (Readiness-Potential)." *Brain* 106 (3): 623-642. https://doi:10.1093 / brain/106.3.623.

LoBianco, Tom. 2016. "Report: Nixon's War on Drugs Targeted Black People". CNN. https://www.cnn. com/2016/03/23/politics/john-ehrlichman-richard-nixon-drug-war-blacks-hippie/index.html.

Lotto, Beau. 2017. *Deviate: The Science of Seeing Differently.* New York: Hachette Books. Mahenthiran, A. 2019. "A Review of the Relationship between the Endocannabinoid System and the Reduction of Depression and Anxiety." *Impulse: The Premier Undergraduate Neuroscience Journal.* https://impulse.appstate.edu.

McDonald, David. 2017. "The Racist Roots of Marijuana Prohibition." Foundation for Economic Education (FEE). https://fee.org/articles/the-racist-roots-of-marijuana-prohibition/.

MD Magazine. 2010. "How Many Pills Do Your Elderly Patients Take Each Day?". HCPLive. https://www.mdmag.com/conference-coverage/aafp_2010/how-many-pills-do-your-elderly-patients-take-each-day.

Morena, Maria, and Patrizia Compolongo. 2014. "The Endocannabinoid System: An Emotional Buffer in the Modulation of Memory Function." *Neurobiology of Learning and Memory* 112: 30-43.

Murillo-Rodríguez, Eric. 2008. "The Role of the CB1 Receptor in the Regulation of Sleep". *Progress in Neuro-Psychopharmacology and Biological Psychiatry* 32 (6): 1420-1427. https://doi:10.1016/j.pnpbp.2008.04.008.

Nelson, Lisa, and Angela Wilson. 2016. "The Science of Yoga: What is Evidence-Based Practice?" Presentation. Kripalu Center for Yoga & Health.

Pamplona, Fabricio A., Lorenzo Rolim da Silva, and Ana Carolina Coan. 2018. "Potential Clinical Benefits of CBD-Rich Cannabis Extracts Over Purified CBD in Treatment-Resistant Epilepsy: Observational Data Meta-Analysis". *Frontiers in Neurology* 9. https://doi.org/10.3389/fneur.2018.00759.

Ribeiro, Luis IG, and Philip W. Ind. 2016. "Effect of Cannabis Smoking on Lung Function and Respiratory Symptoms: A Structured Literature Review". *NPJ Primary Care Respiratory Medicine* 26 (1). https://doi.org/10.1038 / npjpcrm.2016.71.

Schulte, Brigid. 2015. "Harvard Neuroscientist: Meditation Not Only Reduces Stress, Here's How It Changes Your Brain." *The Washington Post*, May 26, 2015. https://www.washingtonpost.com/news/inspiredlife/wp/2015/05/26/harvard-neuroscientist-meditation-not-only-reduces-stress-it-literally-changes-your-brain/.

Sears, Barry, and Bill Lawren. 1995. *Enter The Zone: A Dietary Road Map*. New York: Regan Books.

Sohn, David William. 2004. *Escaping the Labyrinth: Body Memory - The Secret Code That Creates, Sustains and Can Unlock Our Chains*. Raleigh: Life Tools.

About the Author

Entrepreneur, leader, fitness fanatic, healthcare professional, Mark brings a passion and joy for living to everything he does. From the chairman of the board of a twenty million dollar health services agency to a certified yoga instructor, Mark has accumulated an impressive array of diverse experiences. Known for his charismatic, high energy approach to leadership, Mark has led many groups to the successful completion of their missions. Mark's latest endeavor, nurseMARK, is the largest global community of empowered people dedicated to powerful living. Through this community, they are changing the world. Mark is also a leader in cannabis education, teaching people about the beneficial use of cannabis as a medicine. Through his participation in one of the first Master of Science in Medical Cannabis Science and Therapeutics programs, Mark is able to convey the latest research findings in way that makes sense to anyone. In addition, Mark is a voice actor and a CrossFit Level 1 Coach. Mark is most passionate about coaching people on how to live a life they love, an absolutely f**cking amazing life!

Made in the USA
Middletown, DE
19 March 2022

62747117R00078